"*Modern Cast Iron* is a great resource for anyone who wants to bring the spirit of minimalism into the kitchen. With an emphasis on family traditions and a healthy lifestyle, author Ashley L. Jones captures the spirit of having more with less."

—**Joshua Becker, author of *The Minimalist Home***

"Jones is a warm and charming guide to all things cast iron. She has a passion for every detail from the making of it, the preservation, and most importantly cooking with it. Lifelong fans of cast-iron cooking as well as those just beginning their journey will be delighted by her depth of knowledge as well as passion. She does a beautiful job showcasing just how versatile cast-iron cooking is and always has been."

— **Lauren May, Must Love Herbs**

"Indulging the reader's every curiosity about cast iron, Jones delves into the nostalgia and venerable history of cast-iron cooking across continents. Cooking, cleaning, seasoning, choosing pans and even how and who makes cast iron cookware today—every topic is covered in entertaining and easy-to-read prose. Whether because of sentimentality, health concerns or genuine preference, cooking has come full circle back to the days of cast-iron cooking; *Modern Cast Iron* is the how-to manual to pass on to future generations along with your grandmother's favorite cast iron pan."

—**Jules E. Dowler Shepard, gfJules**

"Modern Cast Iron by Ashley Jones has successfully rekindled my desire to try cast-iron cooking once again! After numerous tries and multiple failures, Ashley's stories, practical tips and yummy recipes make me think it's actually more accessible than I thought. I can't wait to add this book to my library and share with my friends!"

—**Victoria Duerstock, author of** *Heart & Home: Design Basics for Your Soul & Living Space*

"Ashley has put together a beautiful book full of practical tips and easy-to-tackle recipes that I cannot wait to try—especially the Crispy Coconut Chicken Tenders! I just flat love this book! The author didn't leave out anything—from how to care for your cast iron to the health benefits of using this precious cookware—and everything in between. *Modern Cast Iron: The Complete Guide to Selecting, Seasoning, Cooking, and More* is perfect for the cast-iron snob to the cast-iron newbie, and I plan to purchase copies for all of the accomplished and not-so-accomplished cooks in my life."

—**Michelle Medlock Adams, author of** *The Perfect Persimmon*

MODERN
CAST IRON

The Complete Guide to Selecting, Seasoning, Cooking, and More

MODERN
CAST IRON

ASHLEY L. JONES

Foreword by
MARK H. KELLY

Photography by
CARISSA FASSNACHT

RED ⚡ LIGHTNING BOOKS

This book is a publication of

RED ⚡ LIGHTNING BOOKS

1320 East 10th Street
Bloomington, Indiana 47405 USA

redlightningbooks.com

Manufactured in China

ISBN: 978-1-68435-102-2 cloth
ISBN: 978-1-68435-105-3 ebook

1 2 3 4 5   25 24 23 22 21 20

Contents

FOREWORD   xi

ACKNOWLEDGMENTS   xv

INTRODUCTION   1

A FAMILY TRADITION   3

A RETURN TO CAST IRON   13

SHOPPING FOR CAST IRON   23

HEALTHY CAST IRON   39

CARING FOR CAST IRON   47

COOKING WITH CAST IRON   71

CONCLUSION   209

INDEX   211

Foreword

ALWAYS REMEMBER:
GONE WITH THE LARD ISN'T THE END OF FLAVOR

Mark H. Kelly
Lodge Manufacturing Company

In the mid-1970s, my father, R. Norwood Kelly Jr., was diagnosed with diabetes. Overnight, my parents switched the family's home-cooked meals from traditional Southern cuisine to an updated version.

Along with a jar of bacon drippings for seasoning, deep-fried foods were gone with the lard. Cornbread, long a fixture on our family's table, was out of favor, and whole-wheat dinner rolls became a welcomed replacement. Olive oil, garlic, sodium-free salt, and other ingredients became the norm rather than foreign elements.

Initially, my two brothers and I wrinkled our noses at the concepts. In time, we learned to enjoy a more flavorful and broader variety of home-cooked recipes than those in the past (not that we didn't slip out to restaurants in Savannah, Georgia, to savor fried chicken and barbecue from time to time).

I won't say that the change in dietary selections was ahead of its time; it was, however, a necessity we embraced for the benefit of my father and our family. Leading the charge in our conversation were cast-iron skillets, griddles, Dutch ovens, and bakeware lovingly handed down from previous generations.

That's why I'm excited about Ashley L. Jones's new book—*Modern Cast Iron: The Complete Guide to Selecting, Seasoning, Cooking, and More*. Ashley's is a much-needed work for beginners and experienced cast-iron cooks. Many of the recipes are updated classics, with Ashley lending her experience and application of ingredients to craft healthier and more enjoyable results.

As difficult as it may be for some readers to accept the concepts presented in this guidebook, I've learned through the years that culinary exploration pays off in new and unexpected heights of satisfaction. And what better cookware to accompany cooks through their exploration than cast iron? With a history that dates to the Middle Ages, cast iron provides cooks with a tool to utilize every cooking technique—searing, baking, stir-frying, sautéing, braising, deep frying, broiling, and stewing—for generations of wonderful results.

Along with allowing the use of multiple cooking techniques, cast iron doesn't require as much oil as other forms of cookware. In many instances, cast iron is the go-to item for fat-free cooking—a feature chefs and home cooks employ as an assist for folks watching their waistlines and calories. And, lest we forget, cast iron is equally at home on the stove top, in the oven, on the grill, and over a campfire with a price point consumers find appealing to their pocketbooks.

One of Ashley's more intriguing substitutions for fried chicken is oven-baked coconut chicken. After the first bite, you'll wonder where this recipe's been all of your life. Dessert is another area where family history maintains traditional ingredients in recipes, with: "If Mama used them, why shouldn't we?" a familiar declaration. Ashley crafts a winner with a blueberry cobbler featuring gluten-free flour and honey that is a tasty update on a classic. And a delightful apple crisp is another twist on conventional kitchen wisdom.

Seasoning and maintaining cast-iron cookware is a topic that's been discussed throughout the centuries of its use. Every brand on the market offers preseasoned items, though some consumers prefer to burn off manufacturers' seasoning and begin the process anew. To assist readers, Ashley L. Jones reviews the use and care of cast-iron cookware with easy-to-follow instructions.

Regardless of the origin of your cast iron's seasoning, the best way to improve the easy-release (nonstick) aspect is to cook, cook, cook, and cook with every item in your collection. Anything prepared with cast iron—protein, vegetable, starch, and sugar emit oil onto the cookware. Heat from cooking turns oils into carbon particles, and each use adds more carbon, enhancing seasoning.

Cast-iron cookware evokes memories of home-cooked meals prepared for every occasion. Other memories recall campfire cooking with scout troops, or fishing and hunting adventures. And many become teary-eyed at the recollection of a grandparent standing beside them as they prepared their first batch of scrambled eggs.

My family's transition from classic Southern cuisine didn't end our love of traditional recipes. It opened the door to more extensive and wholesome selections we continue to embrace. And we share the meals and memories we learned years ago with the children and grandchildren who will inherit our cast-iron cookware and pass them on to the generations that will follow.

Acknowledgments

If writing a book is a journey, then this was a grand adventure. It started with my first trip to New York City and included long road trips, interviews, photography shoots, and cooking experiments, all while I was expecting my first child! I'd like to acknowledge all of you who lent your support and prayers along the way, but that would require a book of its own. You know who you are—thank you from the bottom of my heart!

To my husband, Robby, thank you for your enduring patience, for being my photography assistant, for eating my cooking mistakes, and for driving me all over kingdom come (and not complaining when I had to stop at every single bathroom along the way). You are my greatest support, my champion, my partner. I couldn't do any of this without you, and I wouldn't want to anyway.

To my little son Gordon, you don't know it yet, but you were a big part of this book. Thank you for inspiring me and keeping me on my toes.

To Mom, thank you for always making delicious home-cooked meals for us kids and for teaching us how to do the same for our families.

To my extended family, thank you for sharing your stories of the good ol' days, your knowledge of cast iron cookware, and your secret recipes. Grandma King, thank you for keeping the old traditions alive and for sharing them with us.

To Lodge Manufacturing, thank you for the amazing tour of the new foundry and for sharing your extensive knowledge about cast iron.

To Carissa Fassnacht, thank you for partnering with me on this project. Your photographs captured the beauty and tradition of cast iron dinners.

To my mentor and friend Michelle Medlock Adams and my literary agent Cyle Young, I can't overstate how much your encouragement and support mean to me.

Last, but not least, thanks to the wonderful folks at Red Lightning Books, especially Ashley Runyon for catching my vision and believing in this project. You've all been a joy to work with.

For a list of resources used in the making of this book, visit my website at **www.ashleyljones.com.**

Introduction

Down here in the South, most of us have fond memories of our grandparents cooking Sunday dinners in large cast-iron skillets. Just the look of those dark pans is enough to conjure the smells of fried chicken or roasts and, of course, cornbread—delicious delicacies shared with those we love the most.

During the 1960s and '70s, lighter aluminum and chemical nonstick cookware began replacing heavy cast-iron pans. And as the pots and skillets changed, so did the food. (Good luck making your grandma's cornbread in Teflon pans. I've tried, and it's never the same!)

It's no wonder that folks like me are waxing nostalgic for a simpler time filled with wholesome, home-cooked foods. Unfortunately, our grandparents are passing into history, and most of us have failed to acknowledge—much less document—their vast knowledge of cooking with cast iron. When I realized this, I began asking my own family how to clean and cook in cast iron. Then I experimented with old family recipes, making them my own. What started as a way to reconnect with my own family roots—and recapture those old flavors I missed so much—has become a way of life. I can now enjoy the flavors my family craves while eliminating the risk of harmful chemicals other cookware can introduce.

Whether you're a Southerner born-and-raised, or you're a city slicker from New York, you can make wholesome cooking a part of your family's tradition as you learn the simple secrets of cooking with cast iron.

A FAMILY TRADITION

Home Away from Home

I think it's fair to say that cast-iron cookware solidified my relationship with my mother-in-law.

When Robby and I were dating, I met his parents, Bobby and Mary Frances, during one of their trips to Tallahassee. I liked them instantly and enjoyed seeing them during subsequent visits. But when Robby and I started to talk about marriage, he asked me to travel more than two hours to his family's home in Crestview, Florida. The plan was to spend the weekend visiting with his parents, meeting his grandmother, and seeing his hometown. This was a big step for us, so of course I was nervous!

We got to the house just in time for dinner, and Mary Frances served us Taco Soup. I like a wide variety of foods, but this was new to me, and the mental image of tacos in soup wasn't very appealing. But then I smelled it—the delicious aroma of cumin with pinto beans, corn, and tomato sauce. When they passed around the toppings—corn chips, sour cream, and shredded cheese—all my nervous energy melted away, leaving only a sense of familial comfort. It was like I was sitting at my own mother's table.

I don't remember exactly what Mary Frances cooked the rest of that weekend, but it probably included a roast and hand-picked field peas and corn—the kind of food you hope they serve in Heaven. What I do remember clearly is the cast-iron cookware Mary Frances used with every meal. Those big, dark skillets resurrected memories of my own childhood. I became nostalgic for a simpler time, for fresh veggies picked straight from the farm, and big family get-togethers fueled by down-home cookin'.

Mary Frances and I bonded quickly over food. She loved my appreciation and enthusiasm for her cooking, and she rewarded me with a gift: a small cast-iron pot with lid. She insisted it wasn't an expensive piece, but to me it was priceless. Not only did it represent the bond with my new family but it also helped me reconnect with my childhood by enabling me to cook those same wholesome meals I grew up on.

In honor of her contribution to this book, check out Mary Frances's Taco Soup recipe in chapter 6, "Cooking with Cast Iron."

Reconnecting with the Past

Some deeply ingrained memories can only be triggered through tastes and smells.

The more time I spent around cast iron as an adult, the more I waxed nostalgic. I began to remember countless family gatherings, including those from the summers we spent in Franklin, North Carolina. We would pick veggies in the morning and then sit on the porch watching the rain while we shelled peas and shucked corn. When it stopped raining, we kids would play in the cold creek in the backyard until it was finally time to come in for supper. Those were the simple, languid days of childhood.

At some point, Mom acquired a cast-iron skillet from her mother-in-law. She never did get the hang of frying chicken, but she used that skillet daily to fry or sauté other meats and veggies, as well as cook simple skillet meals like beefaroni for my sister and me.

When we moved into a new house with modern appliances, Mom was afraid her heavy skillet would break the glass stove top, so she replaced it with a lighter aluminum pan. I was thirteen years old at the time, so it's not surprising that I quickly forgot all about growing up on cast-iron dinners.

That is, until the tastes and smells of Mary Frances's cooking triggered my memory.

Perhaps that's what comfort food really is. It's a meal that, through its unique aromas and flavors, brings to mind a happy place and time. It takes us back, reconnecting us with something long gone but still treasured.

I'm thankful those cast-iron dinners have helped me reconnect with my past. I hope they can do the same for you.

A Cast-Iron Contraption

In my in-laws' house sits a small wood stove. Now painted black, the antique used to be a daily workhorse for Robby's grandparents. A few months ago, his family sat down to tell me its unusual history.

Pa and Grandma King were subsistence farmers, which is a nice way of saying they lived off the land and didn't have a lot of money to show for it. They owned about forty acres, on which they grew everything from potatoes to fruit trees, as well as sugar cane, which they harvested and boiled to make syrup. For meat, they raised chickens, pigs, and cows. They also tended to numerous bee boxes, harvesting and selling the honey under their own label.

Pa King was a mechanic by trade, but he could have been an engineer. Back in the 1970s—long before YouTube made homesteading popular—Pa built his own solar-powered hot-water heater out of 4' × 6' sheets of glass and tin that he painted black. A water hose fed into the contraption, which then emptied into a large drum used as a temporary holding tank until the water was drawn into the house. On hot, sunny days, this was sufficient to provide hot water for the kitchen and bathroom.

But the solar panels didn't work well on cloudy days—a challenge Pa King gladly accepted. After a while, he came up with a new contraption, this time using that small cast-iron stove.

Those kinds of stoves were simple in nature. A small chamber in the bottom, called a *fire pit*, held pieces of wood. Once ignited, the wood created smoke, which was ventilated outside the house through a pipe. The fire would heat the entire stove, which then radiated heat throughout the room. Pots and kettles could also be placed on top of the stove to cook.

When the Kings purchased a second, larger cast-iron stove, Pa turned the smaller one into a boiler. Somehow, he drilled two holes through that tough metal. Through one hole, he inserted a galvanized water pipe that was connected to the well. He coiled the pipe inside the fire box and threaded it out the

TOP Pa King's cast-iron stove with a kettle on the burner.

BOTTOM Pa King's cast-iron stove with the doors and vents open—see the holes he drilled?

other hole and into a holding tank outside. Then all he had to do was light the fire in the stove and turn on the spigot. The water would pump through the makeshift boiler to be stored in the holding tank until it was piped back into the house. This system worked so well he later built a larger version with an insulated, fifty-gallon holding tank. This way, Grandma King was able to have hot water whenever she wanted it.

When their neighbors upgraded to the latest glass-top stoves, the Kings continued to use their wood-burning cast-iron stoves. This was how they had lived their entire lives, and they saw no need to change. Plus, wood burns cheaper than electricity. So, the Kings lived like folks did in the early 1900s, right up until 1996 when health reasons finally caused them to move from their farmland to be closer to family.

Pa King passed away years ago, but Grandma King celebrated her ninety-seventh birthday this year. She still loves to garden and prefers to cook on cast iron. Some things never change.

The Sweet Job of Syrup Making

When you think of a kettle, you probably imagine a small pot that is used to boil water on the stove, but the term has been used for hundreds of years to refer to cast-iron pots of all sizes. These were often hung over a hearth or outdoor fire.

However, on eighteenth-century plantations, the kettle was repurposed to render syrup out of sugar cane. The cane stalks were first cut down by hand and then crushed using a mill powered by animals (usually donkeys or horses). Next, the

TOP Robby loved staying on the farm with Pa and Grandma King.

MIDDLE Kettles suspended over an open fire.

BOTTOM Robby's father and grandmother brave the steam to ladle impurities from the cane syrup.

A KETTLE WITH A PAST

My sister's family has a large kettle with a famous past. As the story goes, the Confederates were gathered in nearby Olustee, Florida, waiting for the Yankees to arrive and the battle to begin. During the Civil War, locals were expected to do their part by feeding the soldiers. My sister's great-great-grandparents used their syrup kettle to cook a modest meal—probably hominy, a type of mush made out of corn—for the Confederate soldiers, who went on to win the Battle of Olustee.

cane juice was heated in the kettle, where water evaporated and the juice was clarified until it condensed into syrup.

In the nineteenth century, these kettles were used by subsistence farmers, like Robby's grandparents. Ever the mechanic, Pa King used a mechanical press, powered by a small engine like a car battery and a belt, to squeeze the juice out of the cane. The juice was then placed in a massive syrup kettle measuring more than four feet in diameter. A wall of brick surrounded the kettle and raised it nearly two feet off the ground. Pa King built a fire box within the brick so it could be heated to 227 degrees Fahrenheit. The kettle and its brick platform were sheltered from bugs by a small screened-in building just big enough for the family to stand in while they worked.

And it was definitely a family affair!

Once the kettle was heated, the impurities in the cane juice rose to the top and needed to be removed using a ladle. Since it would take eight hours or more for the juice to cook down to syrup, the whole family took turns ladling the syrup and keeping the fire lit. Their payment: gallons of pure cane syrup to enjoy all year long.

Today, large antique syrup kettles can sell for thousands of dollars. Many are being turned into water features or fire pits. However, few people take the time—or even have the know-how—to make homemade cane syrup. Perhaps we will rediscover this traditional way of life and resurrect it, much like we've done with cast-iron cooking.

FACING The Kings used this kettle to boil hogs and wash clothes. Even though it's much smaller than the one they used to make syrup, it's big enough to hold me (at nine months pregnant) and our hen Lula Bell!

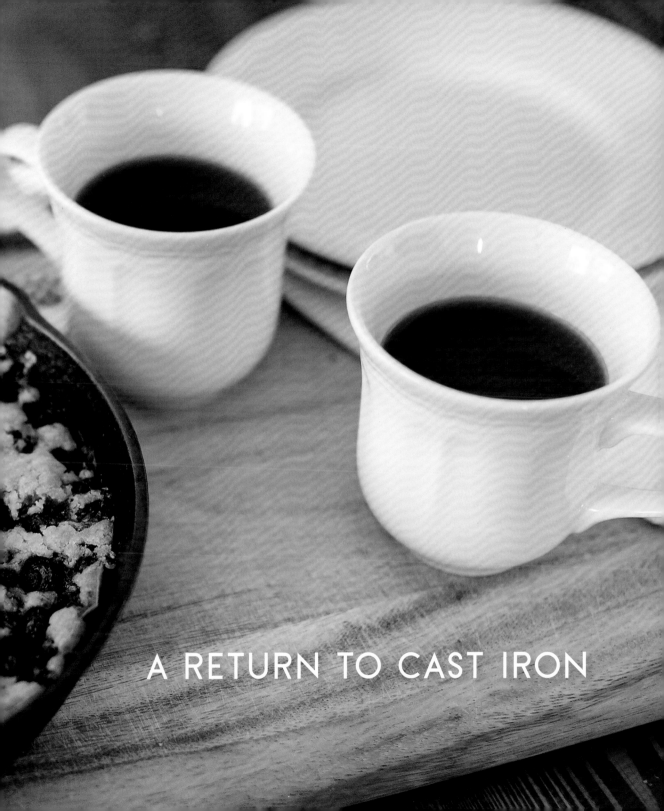

A RETURN TO CAST IRON

The History of Cast Iron

Technically speaking, cast iron is composed of an iron-carbon alloy. It contains so much carbon that it's too brittle to be hammered or rolled into shape like wrought iron. Instead, the metal must be heated over 2,500 degrees Fahrenheit and then poured into a sand mold (or cast) and left to harden. When it cools, the mold is broken, and the pan emerges intact, handle and all.

While cast-iron pans are known as a Southern thing, Southerners certainly can't take credit for them. In fact, the earliest cast-iron artifacts—dating back to the fifth century BC—were discovered in China, where the durable metal was used to make pots, plowshares, weapons, and pagodas. It wasn't until the fifteenth century AD that cast iron was manufactured in Europe, primarily for cannons and shot as well as cookware.

When Europeans traveled to the New World, they brought with them their sturdy cast-iron cookware or "furniture," as it was sometimes called. These pots were perfect for cooking over an open fire, whether suspended by a pole or placed directly on coals. For settlers traveling west, no wagon was complete without at least one cast-iron pot and kettle. Even Lewis and Clark carried one on their famous adventure.

Cast iron continued to be the primary cookware in the United States until the 1960s, when lighter-weight aluminum became cheaper and more widely available. Chemical nonstick pans then entered the market, further displacing cast iron. Later, glass cooktops became fashionable but proved to be too fragile to hold the heavy pots and pans. It seemed that cast iron had become a thing of the past.

But when troubling reports circulated about aluminum and chemical nonstick surfaces in the late 1990s and early 2000s, cooks turned once again to cast iron—the original nonstick pan. As they rediscovered—and shared with others—the advantages of cast iron, everyone from homemakers to college students began to pull out their grandmothers' pans from the attic.

Now there is a veritable renaissance in cast-iron cookware. For years, Lodge has been the only major cast-iron manufacturer in the United States. While it still holds the majority of the market share, start-up companies are popping up across the country. The traditional black pans are also getting a face-lift with new designs and coatings, making them as attractive as they are functional.

It's official. The pan of the past has become a kitchen staple once again.

Today's Cast Iron

The folks at America's Test Kitchen (home of *Cook's Illustrated* and *Cook's Country* magazines) tested bare cast-iron skillets from Calphalon, Camp Chef, Lodge, and T-fal, simulating years of normal household use, and then evaluated each pan in four different areas: (1) browning, (2) sticking, (3) ease of use, and (4) durability. Their favorite was the classic skillet by Lodge. To many, this comes as no surprise.

Lodge has been making cast-iron cookware since 1896, earning the title of oldest and largest cookware manufacturer in the United States. The company has survived two world wars, the Great Depression, the Great Recession, and—perhaps even more impressive—the technological changes that brought us lighter-weight aluminum and chemically treated nonstick pans. This is particularly significant when you consider that its competitors have all fallen by the wayside. In recent years, start-up companies have developed their own cast-iron cookware, but Lodge cast iron remains a favorite among chefs and homemakers alike. In September of 2018, Robby and I headed to the sleepy town of South Pittsburg, Tennessee, to learn Lodge's secret (and to pick up a few pieces for my collection).

Just thirty miles west of Chattanooga, South Pittsburg is nestled in the beautiful countryside between the Tennessee River and the Cumberland Plateau. Rich in coal and iron, it was the perfect place for Joseph Lodge to build a foundry for cast-iron cookware. Although modifications were made to the foundry over the years, the company struggled to keep up with demand. In 2017, the Lodge Manufacturing Company—popularly known as "Lodge"—built a second, state-of-the-art foundry, allowing it to increase production by 75 percent.

Although it's normally closed to visitors, the folks at Lodge agreed to give Robby and me a special tour of the new 127,000-square-foot facility in operation. After several hours of walking the floor and talking with employees, we came away with a deeper appreciation for what goes into every cast-iron skillet and Dutch oven.

How Lodge Manufactures Cast Iron

As America's Test Kitchen proved, not all cast-iron pans are the same. This is a bit surprising considering the process to make this kind of cookware hasn't changed much over the centuries. As we learned during our tour, though, the difference is in the details.

Our tour started on the loading docks where the raw materials are brought in. This includes pig iron, steel scrap, and scrap iron. A large magnetic arm picks up these raw materials and places them in one of two induction furnaces, where they are heated just past the melting point of 2,500 degrees Fahrenheit. It takes so much energy to get the furnaces this hot that the company leaves them running 24/7, even when the foundry is closed.

The molten metal is then poured into a large bin. While workers oversee this process, much of the work is too hot for them to handle up close. For this reason, the new foundry includes a unique robot that looks like a seven-foot-tall silver slug made of aluminum foil. Although it stands on top of the furnace platform, we enjoyed seeing glimpses of it as it worked with surfaces too hot for anyone to handle.

We were also fortunate enough to watch two batches of metal being poured into bins. The metal is so hot that it often sends sparks flying. Called "yellow jackets," these sparks can sting if they touch bare skin, so employees wear special clothing coated in fire-retardant material.

Once the bin is full, an employee pulls it to the side and uses a long-handled rake to remove *slag*—unwanted waste products—from the iron. Our guide told us that slag is composed of impurities that can cause discoloration and even cracking in cast-iron cookware, so it's important to remove it before molding the iron (although some manufacturers skip this step).

Since each batch of raw materials can introduce impurities in the final product, Lodge maintains its own in-house quality assurance lab. There, workers use various methods and tools to test the chemical composition of the raw materials and the iron once it's been melted down. If the composition is off, some adjustments can be made to bring it within Lodge's exacting standards. This ensures the pans aren't brittle and that they don't have weak spots that can lead to damage or poor cooking ability.

Once the quality assurance lab gives the green light, the molten metal is transferred to an area where it can be poured into sand molds. After the metal hardens, the mold is broken and the pan emerges.

Cast-iron pans broken during manufacturing are included with the raw material so they can be recycled.

Steel scrap

Pig iron being delivered

This is where the molten metal comes out of the furnace and is poured into a large bin. The silver robot is barely visible while it works on the furnace platform, causing the yellow jackets to fly.

A Return to Cast Iron

The pans are cleaned of any remaining debris and then transported via a hanging conveyor belt to an area where they're seasoned. Lodge's molding and seasoning processes are trade secrets that are closely guarded. Although we were able to see these processes in action, we weren't allowed to take photos. I can tell you, though, that Lodge uses only soybean oil to season its pans (while some foreign manufacturers are rumored to use inedible chemicals in their seasoning).

The black pans—now fully seasoned and ready for use—are transferred to the far end of the foundry, where employees give them a final inspection, box them, and prepare them for shipment. In this new foundry, it takes only three hours to transform raw materials into finished cast-iron pans, ready to be shipped across the world.

Robby and I drove to Tennessee to learn Lodge's secret to creating the perfect cast-iron pan. Now that we know what goes into each skillet and Dutch oven, I'd have to say that secret is a commitment to excellence. More than just efficient cookware, Lodge creates heirlooms that can be passed down for generations.

Perhaps that's why Lodge doesn't have customers— it has fans! Search for #lodgecastiron on Instagram or Pinterest, and you'll find thousands of pictures of delicious meals cooked in Lodge pots and pans on the stove, in the oven, or over a fire. It seems that for many people, the quality and endurance of these products, and the traditions behind them, have come to symbolize the wholesome American values that make so many of us nostalgic. Then again, maybe people just love the way Lodge's cast-iron browns biscuits to perfection. You be the judge on that one.

TOP An employee carefully removes the slag from the bin of molten iron.

BOTTOM Pans are transported across the foundry using overhead conveyor belts. Cages under the belt protect employees from any falling pans.

After our tour, Mark Kelly posed with me in front of an important tourist spot: the PanMan statue. This stands in front of the Lodge store at its new location next to the new foundry.

SHOPPING FOR
CAST IRON

Advantages of Cast Iron

There are many practical advantages to using bare cast-iron cookware. Knowing these facts can help you make the most of your pans.

Improves with use   Every time you cook in a cast-iron pan, the oils in the food contribute to the seasoning. That means the skillet Grandma uses every day will probably perform better than a new one.

Naturally nonstick   Cast iron is the original nonstick pan thanks to the oils used to cook with and care for it. (See Seasoning in chap. 5 for details.)

Superior heat retention   Adding room-temperature food to a hot pan normally lowers the pan's temperature—but not with cast iron. Once it's hot, it stays hot. This not only affects the cooking time but also helps eliminate hot spots, which can cause food to burn. This makes cast iron ideal for high-heat cooking, like searing steaks.

Heavy   This may sound like a negative attribute, but the weight of the pan helps ensure excellent heat retention. In addition, the heavy lid traps in heat and moisture far better than its glass or lightweight counterparts. (This is why the Dutch oven is referred to as the original pressure cooker.)

Nearly indestructible   If these pans could survive the Oregon Trail, they can survive your kitchen. Seriously.

Easily restored   Don't throw away that rusty pan! You can probably restore it. (See From Rust to Wonderful in chap. 5 to learn how.)

Versatile Whether you're frying eggs or making filet mignon, your cast-iron pan is the perfect option. You can even take it straight from the stove to the oven, or vice versa, which is impossible with most cookware.

Essential If you like to camp or go on mission trips, or if you're prepping for hurricane season (which we do every year), a cast-iron pan is an essential item. It will allow you to cook outdoors over an open flame as easily as you can over an electric stove.

Inexpensive You can get a new twelve-inch bare cast-iron skillet from Lodge for as little as twenty-five dollars. Considering that cast iron will last you a lifetime, and you only need a couple pieces to stock your kitchen, it's much less expensive than alternative cookware.

Modern Cast-Iron Options

Because cast iron is the perfect material for cooking so many dishes, you can find it in a wide assortment of shapes and sizes, from the traditional skillet to Bundt pans. Here's a list of some of the more popular pieces available today.

Skillets Common sizes are nine, ten, and twelve inches, which is the measurement of the diameter of the top rim of the pan (not the bottom). The nine-inch skillet is perfect for pies since store-bought pie shells are usually that size. A ten-inch skillet is plenty big enough if you're cooking for two, but a twelve-inch skillet is nice if you need some more room.

Some nice features to look for are helper (or assist) handles and pour spouts. Remember, cast iron is heavy, so being able to hold it with two hands and easily pour out contents can be very useful. If you need something more compact, Lodge's Dual-Handle Pans provide all the benefits of a regular skillet with two small loop handles instead of the long traditional handle.

If you intend to do a lot of frying, though, look for a deep skillet. These may be measured by the diameter or by the capacity (in quarts).

Griddles You can make pancakes in a skillet, but it's a lot easier to flip them if you have a griddle with really low sides. Round griddles can cook a couple pancakes at a time and can be heated on a single burner. Longer, rectangular griddles hold more food and can be heated over two burners at once.

Grill pans No grill? No problem. With a grill pan, you can "grill" steaks, chicken, fish, and more on your stove top. Yes, you can use a regular skillet, but a grill pan will enable the food to sit up a bit, out of its own juices, and give you those nice grill marks.

If you're interested in both a griddle and a grill pan, you might want to check out the Double Play Reversible Grill/Griddle from Lodge. (I love mine!)

Cornbread pans Here in the South, these pans deserve their own category. Yes, you can make a delicious cornbread in a traditional skillet, but it's more fun to use a wedge pan, which divides the cornbread into eight perfect triangles. My favorite, though, is the cornstick pan, which makes five to seven cornbread sticks in the shape of corn on the cob.

Bakeware It may surprise you, but cast iron's ability to retain and distribute heat makes it ideal for baking desserts. Cake pans, mini cake pans, muffin pans, brownie pans, loaf pans—you can find all of these in cast iron. In fact, Lodge just resurrected its fluted cake pan, which it had discontinued in the late 1990s. This is the first item in the new Legacy series, so I'm curious what will be brought back next year.

Dutch ovens Dutch ovens are essentially large pots that can retain heat and moisture extremely well. Instead of inches, Dutch ovens are measured in quarts. Although five-, six-, and seven-quart ovens are the most popular, you can find them as small as one quart (for serving) and as big as nine quarts or more.

While all bare cast iron can be used over an outdoor fire, camp Dutch ovens are made specifically for this purpose. The food is cooked in one of two ways: (1) suspending the oven over an open flame or (2) baking the food from the top and bottom by placing the oven in hot coals and then adding more coals on top of the lid. This is why camp Dutch ovens usually come with a handle for hanging, three small feet to lift it above the coals, and a flat lid with a brim to hold additional coals. Robby's parents have two camp Dutch ovens that have been in the family for years, and Mary Frances still uses one to make biscuits when they go camping in the fall.

Enamel cookware While the core of these pieces is cast iron, both the inside and outside are coated in enamel, which is essentially a glass glaze. Usually, the interior is a matte white or black, while the outside is a vibrant color.

Since the cast iron is completely coated, there is no need to season the pan, which means you can wash it with soap after every use. However, you'll want to avoid metal utensils and abrasive brushes and cleansers because these can chip away at the enamel, making the pan unusable (because you don't want to eat glass chips).

Since seasoning isn't an issue with enamel cookware, it's most useful when cooking acidic foods like tomato-based soups and casseroles, which can eat away at the seasoning of bare cast iron over time. This is why I have one enamel Dutch oven in my collection, which I use on a weekly basis. (She has such a pretty red finish that I lovingly refer to her as Ruby.)

Since 1925, Le Creuset has dominated the market in enamel cookware, offering beautiful Dutch ovens, casserole dishes, skillets, bakeware, and more. However, Lodge has now released its own line of enamel cookware that is just as pretty and efficient.

You may hear of some health concerns regarding enameled cast iron because lead and other heavy metals are used during the manufacturing process. However, those metals are used to create the brightly colored hues used on the exterior of the pans, not the interior coating.

Rust resistant Have you ever ordered a meal or dessert at a restaurant and had it served in a cast-iron dish? Since cast iron keeps hot foods hot and cold foods cold, they can be ideal servers. However, restaurants use dishwashers to clean their tableware.

With this in mind, Lodge introduced a new line of heat-treated iron. These cast-iron servers are taken through a patented heat-treating process that inhibits rust, allowing them to be cleaned in the dishwasher. You read that right—these little guys can go straight into the dishwasher! Just like regular cast iron, though, the seasoning does need to be maintained.

LIGHTWEIGHT CAST IRON

If you've shopped for cast-iron pans recently, you may have seen some labeled "lightweight cast iron." These pans, which entered the market in recent years, are made of the same material as traditional cast iron. However, the molds used to manufacture the pans are made of metal instead of sand. This allows the pans to be made much thinner than regular cast iron. The pans may also be machined or milled to thin them further.

To lessen the weight even more, the handles on these pans are not integrated like they are on traditional cast iron pieces. Instead, the handles are manufactured separately of other metals or wood and then riveted onto the pan.

The result is cookware that can be up to 50 percent lighter than traditional cast-iron pans, making them easier to lift. But there are drawbacks.

The heavy weight of traditional cast iron allows for superior heat retention and helps with heat distribution. The folks at America's Test Kitchen proved that lightweight cast iron heats up and cools down faster, making it less than ideal for high-heat cooking. It also fails to transfer heat well, resulting in hot spots that cook unevenly.

As for durability, there's no contest. Lightweight cast iron is more prone to cracking and splitting than traditional cast iron, and the handles are more likely to break off.

If you really want to use cast iron but you can't handle the weight of it, a good quality lightweight cast-iron pan may be a decent alternative. However, another option is to simply use smaller pans that you can handle more easily (which is what I do).

Shopping Tips

Cast-iron cookware used to be so important to the everyday home that it was passed down like a family treasure from one generation to the next. In fact, George Washington's mother specifically noted her cast iron "furniture" in her will.

If you're fortunate enough to have your grandmother's cast iron, don't treat it as an antique. Instead, restore it if necessary and use it daily. That's the best way to keep it in prime condition (and honor your grandmother in the process).

However, if you're like most of us, you'll need to start your cast-iron collection from scratch. The good news is that you probably need only a couple pieces: a large skillet and an enameled Dutch oven will do. Between the two, you can make just about anything, including the recipes in this book. Cast iron is also readily available in big-box stores, specialty stores, online retailers, and even supermarkets. And if you really want an older piece that's stood the test of time, you can probably find one in your local secondhand store.

Here are some tips to keep in mind as you shop for your cast-iron cookware.

BUYING NEW

Bare cast iron Look for products made in the United States. It's not uncommon for foreign companies to take shortcuts that weaken the iron, making them more likely to cook unevenly, warp, or crack.

Also, try to determine what oil the company used for the seasoning, as some manufacturers may introduce inedible chemicals.

Enameled cast iron There are so many regulations around the manufacturing process of enameled cookware that there are no manufacturing companies here in the United States to do the job. To make these pans, US companies must work with overseas companies, so don't be surprised if the tag says "Made in China." However, to ensure you're getting the safest, most reliable product, buy from a trusted brand like Lodge or Le Creuset. If the enamel cracks for some reason, these companies are more likely to stand by their products.

Regardless of the brand you choose, be sure to avoid pans with chemical nonstick interiors, even if they have pretty enamel-coated exteriors. What touches your food is always more important than what's on the outside of the pan.

BUYING USED

- Never buy any pan that looks warped or cracked.

- If you see a pan you really like, but it's rusted or has built-up gunk on the inside, it may be a good find if you're willing to put in the effort to restore it. (See From Rust to Wonderful in chap. 5 for details.)

- You may notice numbers or letters on the bottom of the pan. These can represent anything from the size of the stove-top burner the pan was designed for, the pattern the manufacturer used to create the pan, or even the individual molder who made the pan. What these markings will not do is tell you the size of the pan; for that, you'll need to measure the diameter of the top rim of the pan (not the bottom).

- If you see a pot with three small feet, it's a camp Dutch oven. These are great for outdoor cooking, but they won't work on your indoor stove.

- Want to know who the manufacturer is, but it's not listed? That's not uncommon. Cast-iron manufacturers didn't brand their names into their pans for many years. However, if you do see markings on the pan, you can perform an online search to determine which company made it. You may even be able to tell when it was made.

Accessories

There are a few accessories that can make cleaning and cooking with cast iron a little easier. Here's a list of the most common ones.

CLEANING

Scrapers In my opinion, these are a must-have! Use them to scrape bits of food off the pan while it's cold or hot. The polycarbonate scrapers from Lodge are really nice because they're sturdy and have different angles that curve to the shape of the pan. The grill scraper even has "teeth" that fit perfectly in the grill pans.

Scrub brush After loosening any stuck-on food with a scraper, I reach for a brush with nylon bristles to finish the job. A little scrub under hot water is usually all it takes to clean a skillet.

Chainmail scrubber Folks rave about these scrubbers, which are supposed to remove stuck-on food without damaging the seasoning. Lodge's version includes a silicone interior to make it more rigid (like a thick sponge). Personally, I find the scrapers and scrub brushes more than sufficient, but you may prefer the chainmail.

Seasoned Cast Iron Care Kit Lodge has made it easier than ever to care for its cast-iron cookware. It has combined a polycarbonate pan scraper, silicone handle, mini scrub brush, and seasoning spray into a single care kit. The spray is 100 percent canola oil without additives or propellants. I use these pieces daily to care for my cast iron.

COOKING

Silicone handle holders and oven mitts My mom once had a traditional, insulated handle holder melt onto her cast-iron pan—not good! We now use only silicone handle holders, which provide protection up to 450 degrees Fahrenheit and come in a range of colors and sizes to fit any pan. Lodge even sells holders now for its helper handles, which I highly recommend. Just remember to put the holder on the handle before you turn on the stove so you don't accidentally burn yourself.

Since handle holders are not intended to be used in the oven, you'll also need an oven mitt. I suggest one made with silicone to provide extra protection.

Glass lids   Heavy cast-iron lids are extremely efficient at trapping in heat and moisture. When your recipe calls for something different—or you just want the ability to see your food while it's cooking—a tempered glass lid is a great option.

Fry baskets   If you want to deep-fry chicken or make homemade doughnuts, a fry basket can be extremely helpful. Lodge sells various sizes to fit its Dutch ovens.

Splatter screens   Place one of these lightweight screens on top of the skillet while you're cooking to prevent hot liquids from splattering on you.

Trivets   There are a lot of dishes that are best served right from the cast-iron pan (a few of which are listed in this book). However, that means you're going to need a good trivet to keep the hot pan from destroying your dining table or linens. Metal, wood, and silicone are all good materials for trivets. Lodge even offers magnetic silicone trivets that move with your pan (very cool!).

Utensils   Essential items for skillets, griddles, and grills include stainless steel flippers, spatulas, and tongs. One of my favorites is a combination tong and turner, which is perfect for flipping thick steaks or grilled cheese sandwiches. Don't worry about metal utensils on bare cast iron; they won't scratch off the seasoning because it's chemically bonded to the iron. However, you'll need to use wood or silicone when cooking in enameled cast iron so you don't chip the enamel. If you have a Dutch oven, you'll also need large spoons and ladles to dish up your favorite soup or pot roast.

Electric burner If you have any issues with your stove, an extra electric burner (sometimes called a "fifth-eye burner") can be quite handy. My mother-in-law uses hers when she needs to free up some space on her stove top. You can find basic coil and induction burners in retail stores and online for about forty dollars.

Glass storage containers You don't want to store food in bare cast iron because the acids will eventually eat away at the seasoning. Instead, I recommend you invest in at least one glass storage container that holds the same amount as your largest skillet or Dutch oven, as well as a few smaller containers. My favorites are from Rubbermaid and Pyrex.

STORING

Divider pads These soft pads are a must if you want to stack your enameled cast iron. You can also use them in between your bare cast-iron pots and lids to allow air to flow (although a kitchen towel will serve just as well).

ACCESSORIES TO AVOID

Any cleaning or cooking utensil made of cheap plastic These can melt or flake into the pan and make its way into your food. (I've had a plastic scraper melt onto the pan while I was cleaning it, and a plastic spatula melt while cooking. Lesson learned!) Instead, choose high-quality silicone, stainless steel, or wood.

Handle holders with soft synthetic materials on the inside If the temperature gets too hot, these can melt right onto the handle.

Metal utensils in enameled cast iron These can scratch the enamel coating. However, metal utensils are perfectly safe in bare cast iron.

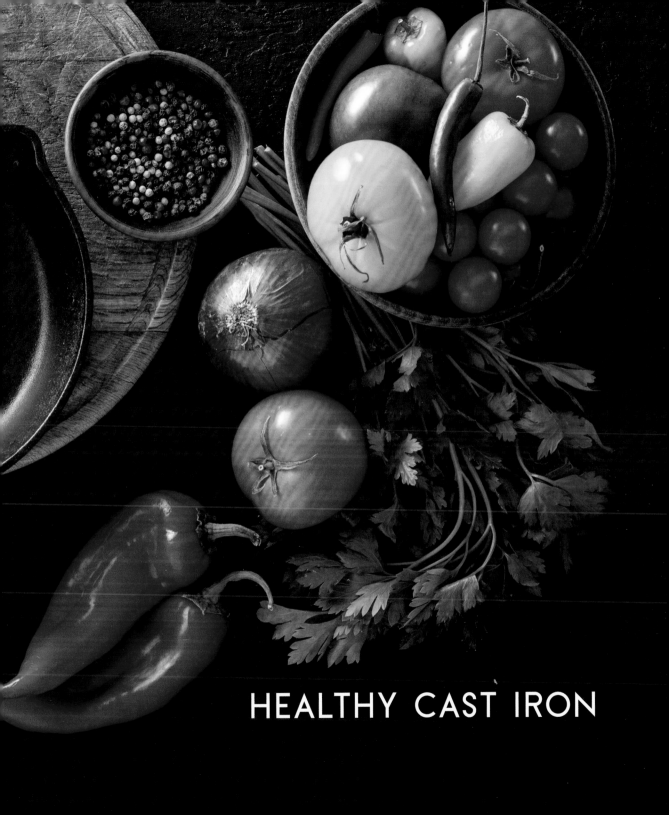

HEALTHY CAST IRON

Health Benefits of Cast Iron

Most of us have never given much thought to the kind of cookware we use. As long as it's affordable and reasonably effective, we use whatever pot or pan we have on hand. But what we cook with is just as important as what we're cooking. That's because every type of cookware has the potential to leach chemicals or metals into our food. The type and amount depends on such variables as the construction of the pan, cooking temperature, cook time, and acidity of the food.

In the case of cast iron, it's estimated that three to four milligrams of iron are leached into eggs, while as much as seven milligrams are leached into acidic foods during the cooking process. Since the recommended daily intake (RDA) for iron is ten to fifteen milligrams per day, depending on age and other health considerations, this is actually a good thing. My family tends to be anemic, so we choose cast-iron cookware specifically for this purpose. (Iron supplements can be hard to digest, so we prefer to get our daily dose in food, not capsules.)

What's more important, though, is what doesn't leach from cast iron, such as the carcinogenic chemicals and heavy metals that are often produced by alternative cookware.

Nonstick Pans Are a Sticky Subject

It's almost a rite of passage. As soon as we have a lease on our first apartment, our moms take us to the nearest store to stock up on essentials. Concerned we'll never eat anything but pizza and Hot Pockets, she buys a big set of nonstick cookware, hoping we'll feel inspired to cook something healthy every once in a while.

But it's hard to cook anything healthy in a pan that can make you sick.

I'm referring to that chemical nonstick coating that's supposed to make cooking and cleanup a breeze. You probably know that you shouldn't use metal utensils or abrasive scrub pads on these pans because they can cause the coating to flake off in your food. However, there are other health concerns you should be aware of.

Invented in 1938 by DuPont, the chemical nonstick coating Teflon eliminated the need for scrubbing and seasoning. While most of the chemicals used to create the coating were burned off during the manufacturing process, a residual amount remained. Over time, an issue came to light known as Teflon Toxicosis, or the off-gassing of toxic fumes while cooking. Short-term exposure of these fumes is known to kill pet birds and can result in flu-like symptoms in adults. However, several of the chemicals are known carcinogens, so many fear that long-term exposure to these fumes can cause serious health issues.

Fortunately, DuPont and several other companies have eliminated the use of a particularly egregious chemical, PFOA, in their manufacturing processes. While PFOA has received a lot of media attention, though, it's just one chemical in a class known as PFCs (perfluorinated chemicals). PFOA may be a thing of the past, but other PFCs are quickly taking its place—and in time we may find them to be just as dangerous.

Makers of chemical nonstick cookware claim their products are safe as long as they're not heated beyond 500 degrees Fahrenheit. However, a nonstick pan left to preheat on high can reach a temperature of more than 700 degrees Fahrenheit within five minutes. Since the type and amount of residual chemicals in each piece of cookware is unknown, and most of us don't monitor how hot our cookware gets on the stove, I don't feel safe using any chemical nonstick cookware.

My cast-iron skillet cooks better, anyway.

The New Aluminum

Around 1970, a Canadian research team believed it had discovered a connection between aluminum and the development of Alzheimer's disease. Although recent research indicates the amount of aluminum we consume in our diets is not a cause of Alzheimer's, many people aren't so convinced.

That's because our bodies have a hard time clearing out heavy metals like aluminum, which can act as neurotoxins, causing a host of health problems such as diminished intellectual function, bone softening and bone loss, and kidney damage.

When people began to look for ways to reduce their consumption of aluminum, cookware manufacturers developed something new: anodized aluminum. The anodization process uses acid and electrical charges to harden the aluminum. Supposedly, the anodized finish will not chip or peel, is nontoxic, and is heat resistant to the melting point of aluminum (1,222 degrees Fahrenheit).

However, even anodized aluminum leaches about thirty-five micrograms of aluminum into your food with each use, regardless of the cooking temperature. While that's not a lot of aluminum, you may want to consider the cumulative effect. That's because we encounter aluminum on a daily basis. Not only is it a plentiful element found naturally in our soil, water, and air, but you'll find it in many household products, from toothpastes to antiperspirants. Aluminum-containing additives are common in baked goods and powders as well, and the metal can leach into foods and sodas stored in aluminum cans. In fact, it's estimated that the average adult consumes about seven to nine milligrams of aluminum daily through food alone (though some baked goods have as much as four hundred milligrams per kilogram!).

If you're looking for a safer alternative to regular or anodized aluminum, there are now many options in which the aluminum is completely coated in nontoxic ceramic or encased in stainless steel. The idea is that your food won't have a chance to interact with the aluminum core at all, eliminating the risk of leaching aluminum.

Another alternative is stainless steel. However, stainless steel products also include chromium and nickel. Although you don't want these metals leaching

into your food, in the right amounts, they can strengthen the steel, thereby reducing rust, corrosion, and leaching. When it comes to cooking, "grade 304" products are considered food safe. These items are typically stamped on the bottom with "18/8" or "18/10," which refers to the amount of chromium and nickel in the composition. For example, a pan marked with "18/8" is composed of 18 percent chromium and 8 percent nickel. When I need to boil noodles or use a sheet pan, grade 304 stainless steel is what I reach for. Otherwise, I stick with cast iron and the occasional glass or Pyrex dish for baking.

The Copper Craze

The latest craze in cookware is copper. This metal is not only a great conductor of heat, but it's also lightweight and beautiful to look at. The problem is that copper is a toxic metal that you don't want leaching into your food. (Copper cookware also leaches nickel, another toxic metal.)

If you want the benefit of copper, though, you can safely use pieces that encase it between layers of high-quality stainless steel. Or you can use cookware that has a copper bottom and a stainless interior. Just be sure the copper doesn't line the inside cooking surface.

CARING FOR
CAST IRON

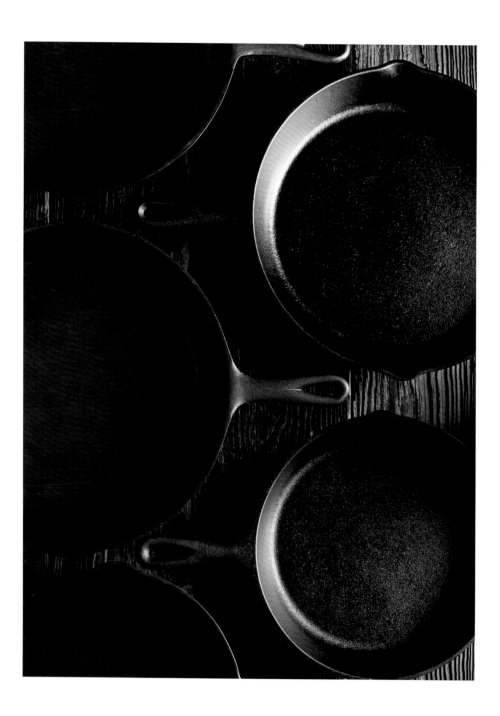

If you're like most people, your main concern with cast iron is how to care for it. That's because rumors have persisted for years that it's hard to clean, easy to ruin, and just plain persnickety. The good news is these rumors are simply untrue.

However, there are a couple hard-and-fast rules you should know. Before you fry your first egg, take a look at these steps on how to keep your black pans in optimal condition.

Seasoning

The trick to cooking with cast iron is to understand—and respect—the seasoning. And I'm not talking about salt and pepper.

In the context of cast iron, seasoning is oil baked onto the iron, which gives it a natural, nonstick finish. It sounds simple enough, but the science behind this process is pretty neat, and it helps us understand which oils are most effective at creating that nonstick coating.

When fat is heated at a certain temperature for a while, it polymerizes, which means hundreds of molecules link together through the formation of chemical bonds. When that fat is heated in a cast-iron pan, it creates a plastic-like layer of large polymers that are trapped within the pitted surface of the pan and are partly bonded to the iron itself. In other words, by applying oil to your pan and then heating that oil, you can create a fairly durable nonstick coating. (Too much heat is a bad thing, though. At a certain temperature, oil begins to decompose and emit harmful fumes. This temperature, called the oil's smoke point, is addressed under Choosing Your Oil in this chapter.)

While all cast iron is sold preseasoned, this nonstick coating is not invincible. Acidic foods, harsh soaps, dampness, and even neglect can reduce the

effectiveness of—or even destroy—the seasoning. That's why it's important for you to understand how to season (or cure) your pan. Through research and trial and error, I've discovered two main ways to season cast iron, giving it what I call a light seasoning or a deep seasoning.

LIGHT SEASONING

You can use light seasoning in the following circumstances:

- After cleaning or cooking.
- Whenever you see dull patches develop on your pan or food begins to stick.

Clean the pan, removing any bits of food and cooking oil. Heat the pan on the stove on medium heat for a couple minutes. Add about a teaspoon of oil to the pan. (See Choosing Your Oil in this chapter for helpful info on which oil is best for light seasoning.)

Wad up a paper towel and, using tongs, wipe the oil around the inside of the pan. Continue to rub oil into the pan as it's heated until the pan looks dark and shiny. Remove any remaining oil residue to avoid a sticky buildup.

While heating, watch the pan carefully and adjust the temperature as needed. Let the oil get to the smoke point, and then turn off the heat. To create a good seasoning, it's important for the oil to reach this point, but you don't want it to continue to smoke. That's because the heat can begin to breakdown the nonstick coating, and the fumes released are toxic if inhaled. (See Choosing Your Oil in this chapter for more information.)

While the pan is still warm, you can rub any remaining oil onto the bottom side of the pan to keep it from developing rust. Let the pan cool completely before storing it.

DEEP SEASONING

You can use deep seasoning in the following circumstances:

- If light seasoning isn't sufficient.

- If you need to season the outside of the pan as well as the inside.

- When restoring old pans.

Clean the pan, removing any bits of food and rust. (For more info on restoring old pans, see From Rust to Wonderful in this chapter.) Preheat oven to 350–400 degrees Fahrenheit. (You may need to select a different temperature based on the oil used. See Choosing Your Oil in this chapter for more details.)

Using paper towels, coat the entire pan—inside, outside, and handle—with up to a tablespoon of oil, rubbing it into the pan's surface. Wipe the pan lightly with fresh paper towels to remove excess oil until the pan looks dry, not oily.

Place the pan in the oven upside down and bake for one hour. Check on your pan periodically—never leave it curing in the oven unattended! If you smell smoke, it means your oil has reached the smoke point. Ventilate your kitchen and reduce the oven temperature.

Remove the pan and let it cool before storing it. This should be sufficient to properly season the pan, but you can repeat the process as many times as needed.

THAT'S NOT SEASONING

When I first started using cast iron, I diligently cleaned it and rubbed oil into it after every use. However, my pans started developing rough patches that caused food to stick. Only after learning about the science of seasoning did I understand what I was doing wrong: I wasn't using heat!

Remember, seasoning develops when fat is heated in the pan, causing the molecules to bind together and form a seal with the iron. If you rub oil into a pan at room temperature, you're simply coating the pan with oil; you're not actually seasoning it.

When storing cast iron, some people also like to apply an extra layer of oil to keep the pan from rusting. This isn't necessary if the pan is properly seasoned, but it's not harmful, either.

SEASONING ON THE GRILL

Some people cure their pans on outdoor grills to avoid smelling the smoke that the seasoning process can produce. While this is certainly an option, it's important to remember that fumes released from smoking oil are toxic if inhaled, and heating oil too far beyond its smoke point can actually degrade the seasoning you're trying to create. For these reasons, I recommend seasoning the pan just below the smoke point. If you do reach the smoke point, then lower the heat or turn it off, whether you cure your pans in the oven or on the grill. (See Choosing Your Oil in this chapter for more details.)

Seasoned Innovation

For hundreds of years, cast iron was manufactured and sold unseasoned. That meant you had to season a new pan thoroughly before you could use it. Although Lodge provided some instructions on how to season its pans, there was a lot of confusion among customers. Finally, in 2002, Lodge developed a way to preseason its cookware, becoming the first US manufacturer to do so.

Not only was this a first in the industry, it was a game changer. After winning one of Good Housekeeping's Good Buy Awards for its preseasoned line, Lodge began seasoning all of its cookware . . . and the rest of the industry followed suit. Now all cast iron is sold seasoned and ready to use (though the methods and oils vary greatly from company to company).

Wondering if your skillet is properly seasoned? Take the fried-egg challenge. Simply fry an egg and gently remove it with a spatula. If it slides off the pan without sticking, your seasoning is just right!

Cleaning

This chapter includes a lot of good advice on how to care for your cast-iron cookware, but there's one hard-and-fast rule: don't put it in the dishwasher!

Why are dishwashers so bad for cast iron? Because they use abrasive soaps that will strip away the nonstick coating. However, that doesn't mean all soaps are off limits. In fact, Lodge specifically states that it's okay to use a mild detergent, meaning periodic handwashing is fine. (I still keep it to a minimum, though.)

Aside from the no-dishwasher rule, here are some tips to help you clean your pan while maintaining your seasoning.

- Keep your pan well-seasoned so food won't stick to it in the first place.

- Use an appropriate oil when cooking. (See Choosing Your Oil in this chapter for more info.)

- When cooking on the stove, adjust the heat as needed to avoid burning your food. Remember, cast iron conducts heat very well, so you should never turn your burner on high.

- As soon as you remove food from the pan, lightly scrape any remaining bits of food with a silicone scraper or a spatula made of wood or metal. The longer food is allowed to sit on the pan, the more likely it will become stuck and difficult to remove.

- For many meals—fried eggs, grilled cheese sandwiches, etc.—you can simply use a paper towel held with tongs to wipe the hot pan and remove any remaining cooking oil and bits of food. No scrubbing or washing is necessary.

- If the food is really stuck to the pan, add hot or room-temperature water and heat the pan for a couple minutes until the food releases. By the time you're putting dinner on the table, you'll be able to pour out the water and wipe the pan clean. (Never add cold water to a hot pan as this can cause the pan to crack.)

- If you have a mess that requires soap, that's fine. However, you may need to do a light seasoning afterward.

- Avoid using scouring pads to clean your pan, as these can erode the nonstick finish.

- If you rinse your pan, be sure to dry it thoroughly with paper towels or a lint-free dish towel. Since the pan may leave a black residue on cloth, you may want to designate a special towel for this purpose. After drying, place the pan on the stove and heat it on medium until it's completely dry. While you're at it, you may as well do a light seasoning.

- And remember—never, ever put your pan in the dishwasher!

Storing

I use my cast-iron pans so frequently that I always have at least one on the stove, ready for the next meal. The rest of the pieces are stacked neatly on a baker's rack not far from the stove. This makes even the heaviest Dutch oven readily accessible.

Now that you've cleaned and seasoned your pans, here are some helpful hints on how to store them so you can get the most out of them.

BARE CAST IRON

- Clean and season the pan, and then let it cool completely before storing it.

- Store in an area without moisture (not under the kitchen sink).

- Feel free to stack (or nest) the pans, as there is no inner coating that can be chipped off.

- These pans can get heavy! Make sure the cabinet, pantry, or shelf is strong enough to hold the weight.

- If you have pans or Dutch ovens with lids, place something like a kitchen towel or paper towels in between the cookware and the lid. (I use doilies and a pretty hand towel.) This will allow air to circulate, keeping the lid from sticking and reducing the risk of rust.

ENAMELED CAST IRON

- Clean and cool the pan before storing. (Enameled cookware does not have to be seasoned.)

- It's best not to stack these pieces, as the enamel can chip. If you do need to stack them, use a divider pad or kitchen towel in between each piece.

Troubleshooting

Here are some common issues you may encounter as you learn to use and care for your bare cast-iron cookware. The good news is that most issues are easily addressed and even easier to avoid.

Food sticking during cooking If your pan won't easily release a fried egg, then it needs to be seasoned. Start with a light seasoning on the stove. If that doesn't do the trick, clean it and then season in the oven.

Stuck-on food after cooking Even with a natural nonstick coating, you may end up with stubborn, stuck-on food. While you can scour your pan, that will eventually erode the nonstick coating.

The easiest way to deal with this problem is to heat water in the pan. While the water is heating, use a metal spatula to gently scrape off the food. Carefully remove the pan from the stove, pour the water down the sink, and use a silicone scraper or brush to finish cleaning the pan. Use dishwashing liquid if necessary. Follow up with a light seasoning.

Food burning If you're constantly burning your food on the stove, start by turning down your burner. Even if you normally cook on high, you won't need to with cast iron due to its superior heat retention. Then make sure the pan fits the burner. Cast iron does not distribute heat as well as some other cookware, which can create a hot spot directly over the burner.

Dark residue Occasionally, you may notice some dark residue on your paper towel or cloth when cleaning and seasoning your pan. This is caused by the seasoning reacting to foods that may be slightly acidic or alkaline. The residue is perfectly safe and will disappear with regular use and care.

Also, avoid leaving food in the pan for long periods of time, as it can draw the seasoning from the pan, resulting in black residue on the food. (I learned this lesson after I placed a skillet with leftover apple pie in the refrigerator, and the bottom crust turned black. It was still edible, but it wasn't pretty, and I had to reseason the pan.)

Sticky residue If you see small bubbles in the seasoning, or it becomes sticky, it's due to excess oil building up and not fully converting to seasoning. This is caused by one of three things: (1) you used too much oil during the seasoning process, (2) the temperature was too low to convert the oil to seasoning, or (3) the time used to season the pan was too short. To remedy this, place the pan in the oven at 400 degrees Fahrenheit for about an hour. Since the pan already has oil on it, you won't need to add more.

Fishy smell Enjoying fish for dinner but want to avoid fishy eggs in the morning? Fortunately, the compounds that cause that fishy smell are eliminated at temperatures above 350 degrees Fahrenheit. Simply heat the empty pan on the stove or in the oven at 400 degrees Fahrenheit for ten minutes, and the funk is gone.

Rust Moisture is like kryptonite for cast iron—just a little bit will cause it to start rusting right before your eyes. Make sure your pans are cleaned, dried, and seasoned before storing, and never leave food residue or water in your pan overnight.

Crusty build-up Over time, a crusty build-up can develop on the outside of the pan. Simply heat the pan in the oven at 400 degrees for about an hour or place the pan directly in a fire until the crust can be scraped off.

Metallic taste If you detect a metallic taste, it means the iron is leaching into the food. While this happens every time you cook with cast iron, the amount can increase with more acidic foods and longer cook times (such as more than thirty minutes). For this reason, chili and other tomato-based soups are best prepared in enameled Dutch ovens.

Choosing Your Oil

If you're like most people, you use the same type of cooking oil your mom always used. If it was good enough for her, it's good enough for you, right?

However, if you're more health-conscious, you may have started shopping for "good oils." Some people classify an oil as good, or healthy, if it's organic and has a balanced ratio of omega-3 to omega-6 fatty acids (like olive, coconut, palm, and avocado oils). Others look for unsaturated oils and those that promise to avoid genetically-modified ingredients (GMOs), thereby avoiding most canola and soy oils.

Regardless of which oils you prefer, though, it's important to keep in mind their smoke points.

An oil's smoke point is the temperature at which the oil begins to break down chemically, causing it to smoke. While this decomposition is a natural process, it generates toxic fumes and free radicals which are extremely harmful, whether inhaled or ingested. (If your oil reaches the smoke point, you'll need to get rid of it—and any food it touched—and start over). One of the main reasons that oil is refined, or processed, is to raise its smoke point so it can be used for higher-temperature cooking. This means that different oils should be used for different temperatures.

Here's a chart of common (and some not-so-common) oils, in order of their smoke points.

Whether you're cooking or seasoning your pan, choosing the right oil is important.

OILS FOR SEASONING

Due to the chemical process involved in seasoning, flaxseed oil is sometimes recommended because its high level of omega-3 fatty acids creates a stronger nonstick coating. However, flaxseed oil has the lowest smoke point of 225 degrees Fahrenheit. This means you'll need to keep the temperature relatively low during the seasoning process.

SMOKE POINTS OF COOKING OILS

COOKING OILS / FATS	SMOKE POINT	COOKING OILS / FATS	SMOKE POINT
Unrefined flaxseed oil	225°F	Sesame oil	410°F
Unrefined safflower oil	225°F	Cottonseed oil	420°F
Unrefined sunflower oil	225°F	Grapeseed oil	420°F
Unrefined corn oil	320°F	Virgin olive oil	420°F
Unrefined high-oleic sunflower oil	320°F	Almond oil	420°F
Extra-virgin olive oil	320°F	Hazelnut oil	430°F
Unrefined peanut oil	320°F	Peanut oil	440°F
Semirefined safflower oil	320°F	Sunflower oil	440°F
Unrefined soy oil	320°F	Refined corn oil	450°F
Unrefined walnut oil	320°F	Palm oil	450°F
Hemp seed oil	330°F	Palm kernel oil	450°F
Butter	350°F	Refined high-oleic sunflower oil	450°F
Semirefined canola oil	350°F	Refined peanut oil	450°F
Coconut oil	350°F	Semi-refined sesame oil	450°F
Unrefined sesame oil	350°F	Refined soy oil	450°F
Semirefined soy oil	350°F	Semi-refined sunflower oil	450°F
Vegetable shortening (Crisco)	360°F	Olive pomace oil	460°F
Lard	370°F	Extra-light olive oil	468°F
Macadamia nut oil	390°F	Ghee (clarified butter)	485°F
Canola oil (expeller pressed)	400°F	Rice bran oil	490°F
Refined canola oil	400°F	Refined safflower oil	510°F
Semirefined walnut oil	400°F	Avocado oil	520°F
High-quality extra-virgin olive oil	405°F		

Flaxseed oil is also one of the more expensive oils, which may knock it out of your budget.

For hundreds of years, folks used animal fats like butter and lard to season their pans. These fats were readily available and used in the cooking process anyway. However, animal fats can become rancid over time, so I recommend you avoid using them unless you cook in your pan daily.

Personally, I like to use vegetable shortening or olive oil to season my pans (with olive oil being the healthier choice). Both are relatively inexpensive, and I use them during cooking, as well. I also like Lodge's canola oil spray, which works great as a light seasoning.

One important note: never use an oil or chemical on cast iron that isn't edible. This may sound ridiculous, but some people recommend using mineral oil, linseed oil, or even oven cleaner. Since any product used during the seasoning process could potentially leach into your food, don't use anything you can't eat!

OILS FOR COOKING

Before you heat your pan, think about whether you'll be frying, searing, baking, or just heating your food. Then pick an oil that best fits the cooking temperature. For example, coconut oil is great for mid-temperature cooking, while avocado oil can handle the higher temperatures needed for searing meats. If you like the flavor of butter (and who doesn't?), its low smoke point of 350 degrees Fahrenheit limits its usage. However, clarified butter (ghee), which has the milk solids removed, has a smoke point of 485 degrees Fahrenheit. This makes it a yummy option for sautéing veggies and searing meats.

You may also want to consider the cost involved. For example, avocado oil would be ideal for frying because it has the highest smoke point in our list; however, it can be quite expensive. For this reason, a lot of cooks use budget-friendly canola or extra light olive oil.

CHECKING AND ADJUSTING THE TEMPERATURE

Cast iron takes a little while to heat up, but it retains that heat very well. For most stove-top dishes, you'll want to heat your pan over medium-high heat for a couple minutes before adding the oil. This helps keep the oil from burning and

allows it to heat up very quickly when you do add it. It also lets you add your food to the pan almost immediately after adding the oil.

If you deep-fry, you can easily keep an eye on the temperature by using a cooking thermometer clipped to the side of a deep-dish skillet. However, it's harder to test the temperature of a thin layer of oil. An electronic thermometer might do the trick—as long as it's giving you the temperature of the oil and not the bottom of the pan.

The best way to gauge your temperature while frying, though, is to keep your eyes and ears tuned in to what you're cooking. Start by heating the pan and then adding the oil. Then flick a little water into the pan. If nothing happens, the temperature is too low. If the water skips all over the pan, it's too hot. But if the water sizzles and then evaporates, the temperature is just right to fry.

After adding food to the pan, listen to the sound it makes. You want a nice, constant sizzling with the oil bubbling around the edges of the food. If there's no sizzling or bubbling, the oil isn't hot enough; turn up the heat just a bit. However, if the oil pops loudly or smokes, it's too hot; turn the temperature down.

Adjusting cooking temperature, especially when frying, is an art form. If you don't get it right the first time, don't worry. It will come more naturally with practice. Besides, you still get to enjoy all the "mistakes" you make along the way!

From Rust to Wonderful

The first Christmas Robby and I were married, his parents gave me two old cast-iron pans that had been in the family for years. Both pans are about ten inches in diameter, but one is a deep-dish skillet, making it a good option for frying. I also received a cast-iron lid that fits both pans.

The Joneses told me how the skillets had fallen into disuse and become rusty, but with some TLC, they brought them back to life. Now they're as good as new… actually, they're better. That's because cast iron only gets better with continued usage, and I've certainly been using mine.

However, the longer a pan sits in the cabinet, the more likely it is to encounter moisture. And it only takes a little moisture to oxidize the iron, turning it into

DON'T CRACK THE PAN

Cast iron is tough, but it's also brittle. To avoid cracking the pan, never subject it to extreme temperature changes, such as placing a hot pan in cold water. You should also exercise care when adding frozen foods—like vegetables—to hot pans. Instead of adding the frozen veggies directly to the pan's surface, add the required liquid first.

rust. The good news is that quality cast-iron pieces are extremely durable and resilient. If you've inherited a rusty pan from your grandmother, or you picked up a piece at a flea market, you can certainly bring it back to life.

In theory, the process to restore an old pan is simple: remove the rust, clean it, and season it. However, removing rust from iron can be a chore. Here are two techniques you can use to lift the rust from the iron.

SCOUR IT

If there's only a thin layer of rust, you should be able to remove it using a wool scouring pad under hot running water.

If elbow grease isn't sufficient, reach for your cordless drill. Most will accept a wire brush attachment, which are relatively cheap and can be purchased at hardware stores. Simply run the brush over the dry pan until the rust begins to lift. (Use the drill without water so you don't get it wet.)

DISSOLVE IT

You can virtually dissolve the rust with white vinegar, but you have to use it carefully. Too much exposure to the vinegar can oxidize the iron further, making the pan permanently unusable. If scouring doesn't work, though, a careful application of vinegar is a good option.

DON'T TRY THIS AT HOME

If you Google "how to restore cast iron," you're going to find a lot of interesting advice—and not all of it safe or effective. Here are a few techniques I don't recommend you try.

Self-Cleaning Some people recommend using the oven's self-cleaning feature to remove rust and baked-on gunk. However, at 500 degrees Fahrenheit, food debris can actually catch on fire! If your pan is gunky, thoroughly clean it before placing it in the oven.

Burning Another recommendation is to place the pan directly in a fire, such as a campfire or within a wood-burning stove. This can be effective, but the extreme heat can also warp the pan. Use this method as a last resort.

Sand-blasting If you have access to a sand-blaster, this might be an okay option. However, the force of the sand hitting the iron can create pits in the pan that may affect cooking.

Electrifying During electrolysis, water and an electrical current (such as from a car battery) are applied to remove the rust. I strongly advise against this method for obvious don't-kill-yourself reasons.

Torching Using a flame torch to burn away the rust might sound like a good idea, but the excessive heat can actually destroy the pan. Plus, it's extremely dangerous. Restoring a pan just isn't worth losing your hide over.

One method is to use a vinegar bath. Place the pan in a metal or plastic tub. Mix equal parts water and white vinegar and pour it over the pan, submerging it. Check on the pan at least every thirty minutes to see if the rust can be scraped off.

Another method includes baking soda. First, warm the pan on the stove for a couple minutes, and then remove it from the heat. Add a couple tablespoons of baking soda to the warm pan, and then add an equal amount of white vinegar. The mixture will begin to bubble as it oxidizes. Check on the pan every ten to fifteen minutes. As long as the mixture is bubbling, it's removing rust from the pan. If the bubbling has stopped, but the rust is still stuck to the pan, add another tablespoon or two of vinegar until the mixture bubbles again. Once the rust begins to lift, you'll need to remove it from the pan.

While rinsing the pan in warm or hot water is usually sufficient, significant rust damage may require a salt scrub. In this method, you'll need to add course sea salt to the pan. Cut a potato in half, and use the flat end to rub the salt into the pan. The corrosive salt will scour the pan while absorbing much of the rust. Wipe out the salt and use the scratchy side of a wet kitchen sponge to remove any excess rust.

If this technique seems to be working, but you need to go another round, take it up a notch by adding heat. First, warm the pan for a couple minutes on the stove. Remove it from the stove and then add coarse sea salt and a tablespoon of oil. Scrub it into the pan using the cut potato. The warm oil will work with the salt to lift the rust.

BAKE IT

If you still can't get rid of the rust, place the pan in the oven (without oil) at 400 degrees Fahrenheit for one hour. When the pan cools, try to scrape off the rust. Repeat this process as needed until the rust can be removed.

You may need to repeat one or more of these steps to lift or remove the iron, but if it's a quality pan, it's worth the effort. Once the rust is completely gone, wash the pan thoroughly and give it a deep seasoning in the oven. The pan should look and work like new.

COOKING WITH CAST IRON

Wholesome

If I had to use one word to describe what cast-iron cooking means to me, it would be wholesome. That's because these black pans bring back memories of family get-togethers surrounding tables burdened with fried chicken or roast, casseroles, pies, and cakes. It reminds me of the hours my grandmother and mother spent in the kitchen, laboring over each dish, sometimes to make it healthier, other times to make it more decadent.

Wholesome can mean satisfying, hearty, healthy, and nourished. But for many of us, eating wholesome food also involves certain dietary restrictions.

About two years after Robby and I were married, I learned that my severe fibro-myalgia pain was largely due to the wheat gluten in my diet. A nutritionist confirmed that my body just couldn't break down the wheat, which was causing painful inflammation. After avoiding wheat for only three days, I felt like a new person!

Still, I suffered from slight nausea on a daily basis, and there seemed to be some lingering inflammation. After a simple test, my nutritionist told me something I didn't want to hear: I wasn't able to process refined sugar. I had already given up regular breads, pastas, and doughnuts, and now I was having to give up sweet tea! I think I shed actual tears.

Then I did what I had to do. I switched to unsweetened tea. I replaced sugar with honey whenever possible. And I limited my post-lunch chocolate to one or two pieces. The nausea stopped and the inflammation disappeared.

Not only did I feel better than ever but the drastic change in my health also made way for one more change: I became pregnant with our first child! Now I have even more reasons to prepare foods that are wholesome and nutritious. And while it's not always easy to cook without gluten and sugar, it's certainly easier than finding something I can eat on a restaurant menu!

If wholesome eating includes dietary restrictions for you, I encourage you to make the following recipes your own. Remember, this is a guidebook on how to cook with cast iron; it's not a cookbook with strict, take-it-or-leave-it recipes. Feel free to substitute ingredients as needed and, if it doesn't work out the first time, try again.

Cooking and eating shouldn't be a source of stress. Instead, it should be a joyful way to feed your body and soul and to bring you closer to those around your table.

Making It Gluten Free

Since Robby and I are both gluten free, I don't even keep wheat products in the house. Instead, I stock my pantry and fridge with various gluten-free options that I cook with as needed. For this reason, I can assure you that you can make nearly any recipe gluten free—and still enjoy it! The key is substitution.

When a recipe calls for regular or all-purpose flour, you can usually substitute it with a store-bought gluten-free mix. My current favorite all-purpose flour blends are by King Arthur Flour (for thickening casseroles and gravy) and gfJules (for baking fluffy breads and desserts). Most mixes tout a one-for-one ratio, which means you use a cup of the gluten-free mix for every cup of regular flour the recipe requires.

Another option is to use pure rice, almond, or coconut flour. However, these are often more expensive than mixes and can add some unintended flavor (unless you want your dinner to taste like coconut). You'll also need to check the substitution ratio; if it's not on the packaging, a quick search online should help.

As for pastas, a lot of traditional brands are now offering gluten-free versions, at least for macaroni and spaghetti. You'll need to experiment with these, though. Some rice-based pastas turn brittle, while some corn-based varieties are too dense. For this reason, I recommend pastas that incorporate multiple nonwheat flours instead of just rice or corn. And if you're looking for something different, the all-vegetable versions made from mung beans, black beans, or lentils are really tasty in certain dishes or even as a side item.

Remember: it's your kitchen, and it's your rules. Experiment with every recipe until you find what works for you—and then write it down in the margins so you'll know what to use next time. And if you're feeling a little glutinous, go ahead and indulge (and enjoy a bite for me!).

The Other Kind of Seasoning

Southern cooking is rich in flavor, but that doesn't mean you need to buy a lot of special seasonings. In fact, the most basic seasonings (salt, ground black pepper, garlic powder, and onion powder) are all that's necessary to bring out the natural flavors of most vegetables and meats. If you're looking for seasoning mixes, though, these are the ones I rely on the most.

Nature's Seasons Seasoning Blend by Morton Includes salt, black pepper, sugar, onion and garlic flavor, celery seed, parsley, and other spices. This adds a light garlic flavor to veggies and casseroles.

Seasoned Salt by Lawry's Includes salt, sugar, paprika, turmeric, onion, and garlic. I use this to season chicken or beef.

All Purpose Greek Seasoning by Cavender's Includes black pepper, garlic, oregano, sugar, onion powder, parsley, and "five other spices" which make this mix truly unique. Sometimes I'll sauté veggies with this or use it to season chicken. However, it's also really good in salad dressing and dips.

If a recipe calls for one of these mixes, feel free to substitute with the basic seasonings noted above or use your own favorite mix. Use those mixes sparingly, though, or you can make the dish too salty.

Choosing Your Pan

In the context of healthy living, wholesome can also refer to financial soundness. I don't know about you, but I don't have a ton of money to spend on dozens of cast-iron pieces, or the space to store them all. In fact, Robby and I have been trying to live more simply, which includes minimizing our belongings to only those items we really need, want, and use.

While you may not be interested in minimalism, you're probably not interested in buying a bunch of cookware, either—and you don't have to. Every recipe in this chapter can be made in what I refer to as a large skillet (ten or twelve inches) or a Dutch oven (five quarts or more). For the instances in which I prefer a small (nine-inch) skillet, griddle, grill pan, or other specialty pan, I'll make a note, but feel free to modify the recipes to work in whatever skillet or Dutch oven you have available. After all, America's pioneers—those original cast-iron cooks—made do with what they had, and so can we.

Cooktops and Ovens

When you think of cast-iron cookware, you probably imagine cowboys cooking over an open fire. It's true that cast iron is still the perfect medium for outdoor cooking, but it works just as well (if not better) indoors—regardless of your cooking surface.

Here's a breakdown of modern cooktops and some helpful hints on how to cook with cast iron.

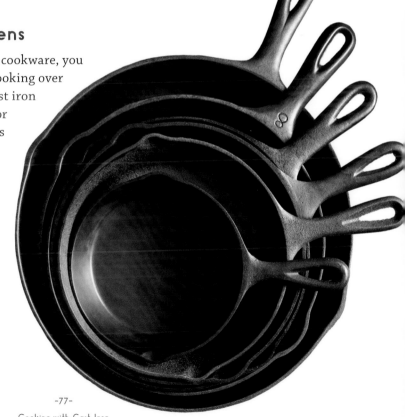

COOKTOPS

Glass While the first generation of glass-top stoves were too fragile to hold heavy cast-iron pots, the newer models are sturdier. To be safe, though, check your manual for weight limits, and don't forget to factor in the weight of the food you're cooking, especially if it's a big pot of soup. To avoid scratching the surface of the cooktop, never slide a cast-iron pan from one burner to another; simply lift it as needed. Since glass tops can heat unevenly and take longer to heat up, you may also need to adjust your cooking temperature and time.

Electric Remember the old stove tops with the electric coils? They may not be as fashionable as glass-top stoves, but they usually heat more quickly and evenly. If you have a stove with electric coils, though, make sure the coils are secure. I almost lost a pan of eggs when a loose coil tipped to the side while I was cooking.

Gas I have a gas stove, and I think it's the perfect cooktop for cast-iron pans. That's because it gives you the most control over the amount of heat you use, with no glass or coils to contend with. The metal gratings over the burners also allow you to slide the pans from one burner to another without concern for the pan or stove. If you're in the market for a new stove, I highly recommend a gas top, whether you use propane or natural gas.

Induction These cooktops use electricity to create a current through a copper wire that is hidden under a glass surface. The magnetic field this creates induces an electrical current in the pot placed on the cooktop, thereby heating the pot. Because these cooktops are extremely efficient and offer great temperature control, you'll see them on many cooking shows (though they may look like simple glass-top stoves). To create the magnetic field needed for heating, most induction cooktops only work with ferrous metals; fortunately, that includes cast iron as well as some stainless steel. So if you have one of these nifty cooktops, go ahead and enjoy your cast-iron pans. Be sure not to drag them across the glass surface, though.

OVENS
Cast-iron pans heat just as well in gas or electric ovens. However, I have seen that dual-ovens, with two separate heating areas, tend to heat unevenly if both

IT'S NOT YOU!

Do you follow recipes diligently, only to have every dinner over- or undercooked? That's because not all cooking surfaces and ovens are created equal. Many recipes you'll find online or in cookbooks are based on cooking times using expensive, high-powered ovens or induction cooktops, which may not be appropriate for your appliance. Take note of how your stove and oven behave, and adjust your temperature and cooking time accordingly. You may also be able to adjust the heating elements on your appliance, but be sure to read your manual and follow all safety guidelines.

are on at the same time. The smaller heating spaces may also complicate matters, so be careful not to burn the top of your casseroles and adjust your temperature as needed. This should go without saying, but never, ever, ever, put cast iron in the microwave.

Breakfast

One of the healthiest things you can do for yourself is to eat a wholesome breakfast every morning. When I was younger, juggling college and work, I ate what everyone else seemed to be eating: frozen pastries, pre-packaged sandwiches, doughnuts, bagels, drive-through biscuits, and (at a particularly low point) chocolate-covered peanuts. I was relatively thin, so I didn't see the harm in it.

It took a while for me to accept the fact that the run-out-the-door-and-eat-in-the-car routine was stressing me out. Worse yet, the lack of real nutrition was depleting me even further, making for long, tired days.

After Robby and I were married, we started having breakfast together. Even if we were too tired to really talk, it gave us a moment to connect before the day began. Eating a balanced breakfast also gave us more stamina for the day and helped us avoid reaching for sugar and caffeine in the afternoon. It was a win-win!

If you're stuck in the grab-and-go breakfast cycle, I encourage you to make a change for the better. Your body (and your hubby) will thank you.

Grand Slam

Eggs are great, but they're even better when they're cooked with hash browns and bacon or sausage. Fortunately, you can cook all these in the same pan at the same time. This helps enrich the flavors and leaves you with only one pan to clean. (Healthy and easy? Yes please!)

Choose a large skillet or griddle and place it on low-medium heat. Add a pat of butter.

Hash Browns Add the hash browns. These can be shredded, in cubes, or in patties, and can be found in the refrigerated or frozen section of the grocery store. I prefer the patties because they're slightly seasoned, cook faster, and brown nicely. If you're using shredded or cubed potatoes, allow a little more cooking time.

Meat Add your favorite bacon or sausage to the skillet. You can use raw or precooked meat for this, but allow a little more cooking time if it's raw.

Eggs Add your eggs last because they take the least amount of time to cook. Simply season with a little salt and pepper and flip once for a perfect fried egg. Or you can scramble your eggs or make an omelet by adding cheese and chopped veggies. You really can't go wrong!

THE PERFECT EGG

Researchers can't seem to decide whether eggs are healthy or harmful. Yes, they are a cholesterol-rich food, but some studies have shown that doesn't impact a person's cholesterol level. Since I have low cholesterol anyway, I enjoy the benefits of eggs: they contain six grams of protein and nine essential amino acids, and are rich in choline, which promotes normal liver function. But what eggs lack is just as important as what they offer: no carbs, sugars, or gluten.

Still, I didn't really appreciate eggs until Robby and I adopted a rescue hen named Lula Bell. She used to lay the biggest, best-tasting eggs I have ever had. Although she's too old to lay eggs now, we keep her as a family pet. She's certainly deserved her retirement!

If you can, choose free-range or cage-free eggs over factory eggs. The flavor is always better, and you'll feel good knowing that the hens who worked hard for those eggs have a good life.

Sausage & Gravy

Here in the South, nothing is better on a cool morning than hot biscuits smothered in sausage and gravy. You can find good gravy mixes in supermarkets, including Pioneer Brand Gluten Free Country Gravy Mix. However, those mixes can get expensive when you consider they just include flour and spices (not to mention preservatives). Plus, you still have to add the sausage.

I recently started cooking gravy from scratch using the following recipe, and I'm amazed at how good and simple it is to make. I recommend country or breakfast sausage, which may be labeled as "pan" or "crumbled" sausage. If you buy it fresh at the meat counter, you can ask for a quarter pound. If you get it prepackaged in the refrigerated section, look for the 16-ounce package. I suggest making small patties out of the leftovers and adding them to your Grand Slam breakfasts throughout the week.

---

1. Place a skillet over low-medium heat. For extra flavor, add bacon grease to the pan. This is especially helpful if you use low-fat sausage, which may not produce a sufficient amount of fat/drippings.

2. Brown the sausage. Sprinkle flour into the pan and stir into the meat and fat.

3. Add ½ cup of milk to start with. Continue cooking until gravy is thick, stirring periodically. Add the remaining milk if you want to thin the gravy a bit.

4. Season with salt and pepper. Serve hot on Traditional Biscuits.

½ Tbsp. bacon grease (optional)

4 oz. (about ¼ package) mild pan sausage

2 Tbsp. all-purpose flour

½–⅔ cup milk or cream

Salt and freshly-ground pepper to taste

Cooking with Cast Iron

RENDERING BACON

Here in the South, bacon grease is an essential ingredient to most recipes . . . but it's not something you buy in the store. The good news is that making—or "rendering"—bacon grease is really easy, and it can be stored in the fridge for weeks.

Start with a few pieces of raw bacon. For most dishes, you'll want regular, country bacon, not bacon with maple or other flavors. Simply cook the bacon on a cast-iron grill or skillet, either on the stove or in the oven. Turn the bacon periodically and remove it from the pan when done. Place the bacon on a plate with paper towels until cool, and then store in the fridge for breakfast.

Bacon grease is solid at room temperature, so carefully pour it from the pan into a glass dish while it's still hot. Once it's cool, cover the dish, add a label, and store it in the fridge.

It doesn't take a lot of bacon grease to flavor a meal (usually one to two tablespoons), so spoon out what you need when you need it.

Blueberry Compote

I love pancakes. Seriously. I wake up thinking about them.

When I went gluten free, I was fortunate enough to find some great mixes, especially Trader Joe's Gluten Free Buttermilk Pancake & Waffle Mix (yum!!). But I had one problem: I couldn't handle the syrup. The combination of carbs in the pancakes and the syrup had a nasty effect on my blood sugar.

Thankfully, I discovered fruit compote, which is fruit cooked down into a type of syrup. In the following recipe, I sweeten blueberries with honey instead of refined sugar, which works great, tastes delicious, and doesn't wreak havoc on my blood sugar. The lemon juice is optional, but it brings out the blueberry flavor.

1. Place a small skillet on low-medium heat. Pour 1½ cups of the blueberries into the pan. Add the water and honey and bring to a light boil. Reduce heat to a simmer and cook for 10 minutes.

2. Gently smash the blueberries using a spatula or fork. Add the remaining blueberries and cook for an additional 6 minutes or until heated thoroughly.

3. Add lemon juice. If you'd like to make the compote a bit thicker, mix the cornstarch and water in a separate bowl and add to the pan during the last few minutes of cooking.

4. Serve warm over pancakes with butter. Store any leftovers in the fridge up to a week.

2 cups blueberries
(frozen or fresh)

3 Tbsp. water

2 ½ Tbsp. honey

½–1 tsp. lemon juice
(optional)

Thickener (optional):
1 tsp. cornstarch

2 tsp. water

Modern Cast Iron

Peach Dutch Baby

Earlier this year, I discovered the amazing Dutch baby, and our weekend breakfasts haven't been the same since. Also known as a German pancake, this treat is thicker than regular pancakes, contains more eggs, and is baked instead of fried on the stove. This is definitely not a Southern dish, though it's almost always baked in a cast-iron skillet. Interestingly, it contains no chemical leavening agents, such as baking powder. Instead, it relies on steam during the cooking process to rise and then falls shortly after it's removed from the oven.

I experimented with this dish for a while before settling on the following recipe. I suggest canned peaches instead of fresh ones because they're sweeter and easier to keep on hand for those mornings you just have to have a Dutch baby. To make it gluten free, I use white rice flour because it seems to rise better than other options. I've also tried it with more flour, but that made it too bready and detracted from the peach flavor. No matter what, though, this dish has always come out deliciously edible, so feel free to experiment!

1. Preheat oven to 425°F. Rub oil into a large skillet.

2. Hand-mix eggs, milk, and vanilla until smooth. Stir in flour, salt, cinnamon, and butter, until blended. Pour batter into the pan. Arrange the peach slices on top. (If the pieces are large, you may want to cut them in half first.)

3. Bake for 15 minutes. Then lower the temperature to 325°F and cook for an additional 5–10 minutes. Do not open the oven door while cooking, as this can cause the Dutch baby to deflate.

4. Remove from oven and sprinkle with powdered sugar. Serve immediately with butter and a dollop of Cool Whip. Leftovers (if there are any) are great the next day.

½ Tbsp. olive oil (for the pan)

3 eggs

½ cup milk or cream

1 tsp. vanilla extract

½ cup all-purpose flour

½ tsp. salt

⅛ tsp. cinnamon or more to taste

2 Tbsp. butter, melted

1 15-oz. can sliced peaches in heavy syrup

Powdered sugar and Cool Whip for serving

Robby's Quiche

Everybody needs a culinary claim to fame, and for Robby, it's his breakfast quiche. He started experimenting with this not long after we were married, and now it's nothing short of breakfast perfection. He even uses a store-bought gluten-free pie shell for us, and it's still better than anything I've ordered from a restaurant.

This recipe works great in a 2-quart Dutch oven because the pie shell is about an inch wider than the diameter of the pot. This allows us to mold the pie shell up the sides of the pot a bit, creating the flaky crust for the sides of the quiche. If you use a regular skillet or larger Dutch oven, use two pie shells to cover the bottom of the pan and create the sides. Don't be afraid to tear apart the shells and mold them to the shape of the pan you're using.

1. Preheat oven to 400°F.

2. Rub oil into a small Dutch oven. Place one pie shell in the bottom of the Dutch oven, molding it up the sides. Use the second pie shell if needed.

3. Add all ingredients to a large bowl and mix well. Pour the mixture into the pie shell.

4. Bake uncovered for 1 hour or until done. Serve hot or cold with a side of fruit.

½ Tbsp olive oil (for the Dutch oven)

1–2 frozen deep-dish pie shells (defrosted)

5 eggs

1 cup cheddar cheese, shredded

½ small onion, chopped

1 cup broccoli, chopped (frozen or fresh)

1 package Canadian bacon, diced

¼ cup cream

Seasoning to taste (Morton's Nature's Seasons Seasoning Blend, garlic powder)

Homemade Biscuits

As a child, I loved to hear the sound of Mom opening a Pillsbury can, the kind you have to bang on the edge of the counter until it goes "POP!" If we were having breakfast, we would coat the buttered biscuits in jelly, apple butter, or honey, or slather them in gravy. For dinner, we often enjoyed savory garlic cheddar biscuits. And for dessert—my favorite—we would drizzle Hershey's syrup on plain, buttered biscuits. I still crave those from time to time.

I always enjoyed fresh-from-the-oven biscuits, but my mother never made them from scratch. She claimed they never turned out as good as Grandma's biscuits, but I'm not so sure about that. Either way, we stuck with the easy-to-make goodness of Pillsbury.

If you still like to make those heat-and-serve biscuits, that's fine! Simply use your cast-iron skillet or griddle to bake them to perfection, with just the right amount of crunch on the outside and a soft, flaky inside. For even more golden crunch, make sure you preheat and oil the pan and leave some room in between the biscuits to allow air to circulate.

As much as I'd like to pop open one of those cans today, they've yet to come out with a gluten-free option. Thankfully, though, there are gluten-free biscuit mixes available now. Some are pretty good, but they can get expensive, and I don't like the preservatives they often include.

So this year, fueled by pregnancy cravings, I felt compelled to dive into the art of biscuit-making. After a bit of research and much trial and error (think: hard hockey pucks), I finally settled on the following old-time recipes. I can tell you from experience that these turn out just as delicious if you use regular or gluten-free flour.

These biscuits may not make a "popping" noise, but they sure make me proud when they come out of the oven.

TO PREHEAT OR NOT

In several of the following recipes, I've noted that the pan should be preheated in the oven. This is especially helpful with baked goods, making the bottom nice and crispy. However, preheating is an optional step you can skip, especially if you don't want the food to be too crispy or if you're trying to avoid burning, as in the case of cornsticks.

Experiment with each recipe to see if you prefer the pan preheated or not.

Traditional Biscuits

The following is a traditional biscuit recipe that requires the dough to be rolled out and cut into circular shapes before baking. These take a little more work than a drop biscuit, but if you're jonesing for your grandma's biscuits, they're worth the effort.

_____

1. Preheat oven to 450°F. Place a large skillet in the oven for 3 minutes to preheat.

2. Meanwhile, lightly flour a wood cutting board or parchment paper.

3. Remove the pan from the oven, and add a light coating of oil using tongs to protect your fingers.

4. Add dry ingredients to a large bowl and stir together. Work in the shortening with your fingers. Add the milk slowly, stirring with a fork. The dough should be soft but not sticky. Once it separates from the sides of the bowl, stop mixing it.

5. Place the dough on the cutting board and roll or pat it lightly until it's about ¾ inches thick. Be careful not to get the dough too thin. Cut out the biscuits using a floured biscuit cutter or small glass.

6. Place the biscuits on the hot pan. Bake for 15–18 minutes or until golden brown.

1½ Tbsp. oil
(for the skillet)

2 cups self-rising flour

½ tsp. salt

3 Tbsp. vegetable shortening

¾ cup milk

SAVORY BISCUITS

If you're looking for something a little more savory, add your favorite ingredients like garlic, oregano, and cheese to the batter, and bake as directed.

Cooking with Cast Iron

Buttermilk Pour Biscuits

Although our grandparents may have loved buttermilk, it's not something we typically drink anymore. Instead, we prefer cow's milk, or what our grandparents called sweet milk. However, buttermilk still has a prominent place in the world of baking. That's because its acidic nature makes extra-fluffy biscuits, pancakes, and more.

In the following recipe, the batter is a bit too soupy to be rolled like traditional biscuits or dropped on a skillet. Instead, I prefer to pour it into a cast-iron muffin pan or mini cake pan, which is why I call it a pour biscuit.

---

1. Preheat oven to 450°F. Place a muffin pan in the oven for 3 minutes to preheat. Then, remove the pan from the oven and add a light coating of oil using tongs to protect your fingers.

2. In a large bowl, stir all dry ingredients together. Add the butter, cutting it into the flour with a fork until coarse and crumbly. Stir in the lemon juice and buttermilk until blended. The mixture will be a bit soupy.

3. Pour the batter into the pan and bake for 25–30 minutes or until golden brown.

½ Tbsp. oil (for the pan)

2 cups all-purpose flour

1 Tbsp. baking powder

¼ tsp. baking soda

2 tsp. sugar

¼ tsp. salt

½ cup unsalted butter, softened but not melted

1 tsp. lemon juice

1 ¾ cups buttermilk

BUTTERMILK SKILLET BISCUIT

In the spirit of minimalism, I experimented with baking the Buttermilk Pour Biscuits in a standard skillet. The result is something that looks like cornbread but tastes like a biscuit—delicious! This is a great option if you're craving buttermilk biscuits, you're low on time, and you only have a skillet to work with. It's also great on any Saturday morning with a heaping helping of sausage and gravy.

To make, prepare the batter using the recipe above, but decrease the buttermilk to 1 ½ and use an oiled, preheated skillet instead of a muffin or mini cake pan. Cut the biscuit into wedges like cornbread and serve with all the fixin's a good biscuit deserves.

Modern Cast Iron

Mayonnaise Biscuits

If you weren't raised on mayonnaise rolls, they may sound a bit weird. However, mayonnaise is made of oil and eggs, the perfect ingredients to bake fluffy rolls or biscuits.

    This recipe for drop biscuits comes from my grandmother. In my mother-in-law's version (see the recipe for Mayonnaise Rolls in the variation that follows) the batter is placed in a muffin tin, so we call them rolls instead of biscuits. Both are delicious and easy to make and can be modified from sweet to savory. These might end up being your go-to biscuits for breakfast and dinner.

1. Preheat oven to 425°F. Place a large skillet in the oven for 3 minutes to preheat. Then remove the pan from the oven and add a light coating of oil using tongs to protect your fingers.

2. Place flour in a large bowl. In a separate bowl, whisk together mayonnaise and milk until smooth. Stir the mixture into the flour until blended, but avoid overworking the batter. The consistency should be thick.

3. Using your hands, roll the batter into 12 small balls, and drop them into the hot pan. Moisten your fingertips with water periodically to keep the batter from sticking while working with it.

4. Place the pan back in the oven and bake for 25–30 minutes or until golden brown.

½ Tbsp. oil (for the pan)

2 cups self-rising flour

4 Tbsp. regular mayonnaise (not low fat or vegan)

1 cup milk

MAYONNAISE ROLLS

Although quite similar, my mother-in-law's Mayonnaise Rolls are a bit sweeter and lighter than the Mayonnaise Biscuits.

    Follow the same preparation directions as above. Spoon the batter into a preheated, oiled muffin pan and bake at 350°F until golden brown.

½ Tbsp. oil (for the pan)

1 ½ cups self-rising flour

2 Tbsp. regular mayonnaise (not low-fat or vegan)

2 Tbsp. sugar

1 cup milk

milk. Sometimes they were sweetened or served with molasses, maple syrup, gravy, or baked beans. Here in the South, johnnycakes were supposedly made with flour instead of cornmeal, differentiating them from the traditional hoe cakes.

The following are the basic recipes for hoe cakes and corn pone if you're interested in trying these old-time favorites. However, if you're looking for something a bit more . . . tasty . . . skip over to Cornbread, Cornsticks, and Corn Muffins.

Hoe Cake

1. Place a skillet over medium heat.

1 cup cornmeal

⅓–½ cup water

2. Place the cornmeal in a bowl, and add the water a little bit at a time while stirring. The consistency should be rather thick. Patty out the cornmeal into small pancakes.

3. Add the hoe cakes to the skillet (without oil). Cook the cakes until crispy, flipping periodically. Serve hot.

Corn Pone

1. Start with the recipe for Hoe Cakes, and add 1 teaspoon of salt and 2 tablespoons of bacon grease to the mix. Patty into pancakes and panfry with oil until crispy.

2. Another option is to pour the batter into a greased skillet and bake at 450°F for about 15 minutes or until golden brown.

CORNBREAD, CORNSTICKS, AND CORN MUFFINS

No family or church dinner is served in the South without a side of hot cornbread baked in a cast-iron skillet . . . not without raising some eyebrows, anyway.

A big step up from corn pone, cornbread includes eggs and milk but omits the bacon grease. Traditionally, Southern cornbread used white cornmeal, while other parts of the country preferred yellow cornmeal and added sugar and flour. Here in the South, we still prefer our cornbread straight up, but the sweetened variety can add a nice touch to spicy dinners or serve as a not-too-sweet dessert, especially if served as corn muffins.

While cornbread is usually baked in a cast-iron skillet, cornstick pans form the bread into corn-on-the-cob shapes, which are lots of fun for kids and adults alike. Both Robby's and my grandparents used to dip cornsticks in buttermilk or sweet milk for a late-night snack that was easy on the stomach. You can enjoy them with butter, though, if you prefer.

Southern Cornbread

1. Preheat oven to 450°F. Place a large skillet in the oven for 3 minutes to preheat. Then remove the pan from the oven and add a light coating of oil, using tongs to protect your fingers.

2. In a large bowl, mix the cornmeal and egg. Stir in the buttermilk a little at a time until the batter is very thin.

3. Pour batter into the greased skillet and bake for 20 minutes or until golden brown.

½ Tbsp. oil (for the pan)

1 cup white self-rising cornmeal

1 egg

1 cup buttermilk

Sweetened Cornbread

1. Preheat oven to 425°F. Place a large skillet in the oven for 3 minutes to preheat. Remove the pan and add a light coating of oil, using tongs to protect your fingers.

2. In a large bowl, mix the dry ingredients and egg with a fork. Add milk and blend until smooth.

3. Pour batter into the greased skillet and bake for 20 minutes or until golden brown.

½ Tbsp. oil (for the pan)

1 ⅔ cup self-rising cornmeal (white or yellow)

½ cup sugar

¼ cup all-purpose flour

1 tsp. baking powder

1 egg

1 ¼ cups milk

CORNSTICKS AND CORN MUFFINS

You can make cornsticks using either of the recipes above, but they must be baked in a cast-iron cornstick pan. For Corn Muffins, use the Sweetened Cornbread recipe and bake in a cast-iron muffin pan.

Because the molds in both pans are shallow, you'll need to take care not to burn the cornbread: skip the preheating step, oil the pan thoroughly, and reduce the cooking time as needed. Carefully remove the baked cornbread and serve hot with butter.

Modern Cast Iron

Appetizers

Appetizers are a great way to keep your guests or family content while they're waiting for the main dish. Since apps are usually pretty quick and easy to make, they're also ideal for potlucks and parties or just a Friday evening at home watching the TV.

Most appetizers are best served hot, and nothing keeps food hot like cast iron. In this section, I've included two recipes to give you an idea of how to use the same skillet to cook and serve appetizers. After you've tried these, pull out your favorite appetizer recipes and make them in your cast-iron pan. Who knows? Maybe you'll even get a bite before it's all gone.

TACO SEASONING

Those taco seasoning packets are tasty and relatively inexpensive, but you can make a healthier version at home with less salt and no preservatives. This homemade version is also easy to modify, allowing you to make spicier or milder dishes as needed.

As for the cost, you probably have these ingredients on hand already, which will save you a little money. If you do need to buy a spice, though, check out the Mexican or international aisle in your supermarket. The spices there are often significantly cheaper than the name-brand versions in the spice aisle.

COMBINE:

2 tsp. chili powder

1 ½ tsp. ground cumin

½ tsp. paprika

½ tsp. crushed red pepper

½ tsp. salt

¼ tsp. garlic powder

¼ tsp. onion powder

¼ tsp. dried oregano

¼ tsp. black pepper

1 Tbsp. all-purpose flour as thickener (optional)

Layered Nachos

You just can't go wrong with nachos. But in this recipe, they're taken to the next level by layering hearty beef and cheese with tortilla chips and then baking in the goodness. Use a deep skillet for this if you have one, and be sure to serve the nachos in the skillet so they stay hot.

1. Preheat the oven to 400°F.

2. Place a large skillet over medium heat. Brown beef with the onion and taco seasoning until done. Turn off the heat and drain any excess grease.

3. Scoop out the beef and place in a bowl. Mix in 1 cup of shredded cheese.

4. Add a layer of tortilla chips to the hot skillet. Then spoon on a layer of the beef and cheese mixture. Add one or two more layers, alternating between tortilla chips and the beef and cheese mixture. Top with a layer of shredded cheese and jalapeños.

5. Bake the nachos for 10–15 minutes, until the cheese melts and begins to brown.

6. Top with fresh tomatoes and scallions. Serve in the pan with sides of fresh salsa, sour cream, and extra cheese.

½ lb. ground beef

¼ onion, chopped

1 packet of taco seasoning

2 cups shredded cheese (Monterey Jack, sharp cheddar, or a mixture)

1 bag tortilla chips (flour or corn)

1 jalapeño pepper, sliced

1 small tomato, chopped

2 scallions, chopped

Fresh salsa and sour cream for serving

Spinach Casserole

My mom and I aren't big fans of spinach, so when she made this spinach casserole for a family dinner, I knew it had to be something special—and it is! The combination of cream of mushroom soup and cream cheese takes away the bitterness of the spinach, while the French-fried onions give it flavor and a satisfying crunch that'll make you want to eat the whole pan. Serve this in the hot skillet to keep it warm or enjoy leftovers right out of the fridge.

---

1. Preheat oven to 350°F.

2. Thaw and drain the spinach. Use paper towels or a cotton cloth to wring the spinach and remove the remaining moisture.

3. Mix together the soup and cream cheese in a microwave-safe bowl and microwave 1 ½ minutes or until warm. Combine the soup and cream cheese mixture with the spinach and stir in 1 cup of the onions.

4. Place the mixture in a small skillet, and top with the remaining ½ cup of onions. Bake for 20 minutes.

5. Serve hot with crackers.

1 10-oz. package chopped spinach, frozen

1 10.5-oz. can condensed cream of mushroom soup

1 8-oz. package cream cheese

1 ½ cups French-fried onions

Cooking with Cast Iron

Sides

Side items are taken to a whole new level here in the South. In fact, with sides like macaroni and cheese, field peas, and collard greens, you may decide to skip the main dish altogether.

In this section, you'll learn how to cook these classics and more using such basics as bacon, chicken broth, and beef consommé. If you're low on broth or consommé, or you want to make the flavor even richer, try my secret ingredients: Better than Bouillon Beef Base and Chicken Base. These jars of condensed bouillon have a bolder taste than the dried cubes and contain less salt. I always keep a jar of each in the fridge.

Not every side has to be savory, though. If you're looking for something to cure your sweet tooth, check out the recipes for Papa's Sweet Potato Casserole and Maduros. They might have you skipping dessert as well as dinner.

DEGLAZING

You know those little bits of food that stick to the bottom of the skillet or Dutch oven when you sauté or roast meat? Those are actually caramelized drippings from the juices of the meat, known as fond. To release their flavor, simply add a bit of liquid to the pan while it's being heated. Then scrape the bottom with a spatula for a few seconds until the crusty bits are dissolved into the liquid. This process, called deglazing, is a great way to maximize flavor in your dish or to start a gravy.

Collard Greens

No Southern gathering is complete without a side of greens. Since collard greens have a milder flavor than turnip greens, they're the favorite among my family. Greens are often cooked with ham hocks, but I find it easier—and just as delicious—to use bacon. I also appreciate that bacon contains less salt than ham hocks.

Grocery stores sell fresh, chopped collard greens by the bag, but these tend to have a lot of stem pieces. The frozen packages are fine in a pinch, but the texture and flavor are never as good as fresh greens. If you have the time, buy a mess (that's Southern for "a bunch" or "a bundle") of fresh leafy collards, and clean and cut them yourself.

When cooking greens, keep in mind that the liquid in the pot is just as important as the greens themselves. Called potlicker (also spelled pot licker, pot lickr, pot likker, and pot liquor), this broth is either served up in a bowl with the greens or by itself as an appetizer. It is always served with Southern cornbread, which is used to soak up every drop of potlicker.

1. Place a large Dutch oven over low-medium heat.

2. Render the bacon in the Dutch oven until it's crispy. Add the chicken broth, and deglaze the Dutch oven.

3. Add the collard greens, followed by enough water to cover the greens. Season and simmer for 45 minutes to an hour or until tender.

4. Serve steaming hot in a bowl with lots of potlicker, a side of fresh Cornbread, and a bottle of Crystal brand hot sauce.

3–4 pieces bacon, regular flavor

1 14.5-oz. can chicken broth

1 mess fresh collard greens, cleaned and cut into pieces

Seasoning to taste (Morton's Nature's Seasons Seasoning Blend, garlic powder)

Cooking with Cast Iron

Modern Cast Iron

Baby Limas

Not all lima beans are created equal. If you've ever had the large ones and didn't care for them, try this recipe for baby limas. Also known as green limas, these have a milder flavor than the larger variety and are sure to win over even the pickiest eater.

The following recipe came from my sister Madeline, who is quite the cook. She helped me realize the importance of each ingredient and step. For example, if you don't render the bacon until it's crispy, you'll end up boiling it in the broth, which doesn't provide as much flavor. You'll have the same problem if you dilute the chicken broth with water. And the seasoning? I've listed my favorites, but you can substitute as needed. Just don't add a lot of salt, because chicken broth tends to be salty.

---

1. Place a large Dutch oven over low-medium heat.

2. Render the bacon in the Dutch oven, cooking it until it becomes crispy. Add chicken broth, and use it to deglaze the Dutch oven. Add the lima beans, and season well.

3. Simmer at least 1 hour or until tender. Serve hot, preferably with cornbread.

4 strips bacon, regular flavor

2 14.5-oz. cans chicken broth

1 32-oz. bag baby lima beans, frozen

Seasoning to taste (Lawry's Seasoned Salt, Cavender's All Purpose Greek Seasoning, garlic powder, black pepper)

Field Peas

You've probably had black-eyed peas on New Year's Day, but what about zipper, purple hull, crowder, or iron clay peas? All of these are unique varieties of what are commonly called field peas. Sometimes they're simply labeled "field peas," but you may find specific varieties in your local farmer's market or supermarket. Taste for yourself, and make a note of which kinds you like the most so you can search for them next time they're in season.

The following is a basic recipe that will allow you to prepare any variety of field pea, whether they're fresh, frozen, or dried. If you use fresh peas, feel free to leave in some of the softer pea pods, called snaps. If you use dried peas, don't worry about soaking them overnight; one of the nice things about field peas is that they're softer than other legumes, so soaking is unnecessary.

---

1. Place a large Dutch oven over low-medium heat. Render the bacon in the Dutch oven until it's crispy. Add 1 can of chicken broth, and use it to deglaze the Dutch oven.

2. Add field peas. If making a large amount, you may want to add the second can of chicken broth. Top with enough water to cover the peas. Season and simmer until tender, about 45 minutes to an hour, depending on whether the peas were fresh, frozen, or dried.

2–4 strips bacon, regular flavor

1–2 14.5-oz. cans chicken broth

1 mess field peas, rinsed

Seasoning to taste (Morton's Nature's Seasons Seasoning Blend, garlic powder, black pepper)

Modern Cast Iron

Homemade Mac & Cheese

One of my favorite foods as a child was Ginger's (my sister's grandmother) homemade macaroni and cheese, but when I set out to make it in a Dutch oven, I wasn't sure I could pull it off.

For one thing, Ginger cooks everything she can in cast iron—but she's always made her macaroni and cheese in a glass baking dish. I wasn't sure how the change in cookware would affect the final result. I ended up selecting an enameled Dutch oven, and I'm glad I did. Although the gooey cheese stuck to the side of the pot, we were able to soak it overnight (something you can't do with bare cast iron). If you don't have an enameled Dutch oven, you can use a regular Dutch oven or even a deep skillet; just be sure to oil it well before adding the macaroni.

Ginger also used a high-quality red rind (hoop) cheese, which provided a strong, rich flavor and melted down nicely. Since this is hard to find today, I substituted freshly shredded mild cheddar and Colby-jack, which worked great.

I wasn't sure I could reinvent Ginger's macaroni and cheese, but with a little experimentation, I think I nailed it.

---

1. Preheat oven to 375°F.

2. Use paper towels to oil the inside of a large enameled Dutch oven.

3. Boil the macaroni in a separate pot. Meanwhile, mix the eggs, milk, cream, and cheese in a large bowl. Stir in the cooked macaroni, salt, and most of the pepper. The consistency will be soupy.

4. Pour the macaroni mixture into the Dutch oven, and top with a liberal amount of ground pepper. Bake uncovered for 1 hour to 1 hour and 15 minutes or until the macaroni is set and no longer runny.

2 tsp oil

1 12-oz. box elbow macaroni, cooked

5 eggs

2 12-oz. cans evaporated milk

¾ cup cream or regular milk

2 lbs. cheese (red rind/hoop, mild cheddar, and/or Colby-jack), shredded

½ Tbsp. salt

½ Tbsp. freshly-ground pepper

Garlic Potatoes

I've never met a potato I didn't like, especially one covered in garlic. But if you want your taters to have the perfect texture—firm on the outside, soft on the inside—then you have to bake them in cast iron.

In the following recipe, I use yellow Yukon potatoes, which are soft and buttery. However, you can use any variety of potato you prefer. I use a small 2-quart Dutch oven for this, but you can use a bigger one or even a deep-dish skillet.

---

1. Preheat oven to 350°F.

2. Use paper towels to oil the inside of a Dutch oven.

3. In a large bowl, toss potatoes, onion, and garlic in the olive oil. Season to taste. Place the potatoes in the Dutch oven, and bake uncovered for 50 minutes or until tender.

½ Tbsp. oil (for the Dutch oven)

1 lb. yellow Yukon potatoes, cubed

1 sweet onion, cubed

3 or more garlic cloves, cut in half

1 Tbsp. olive oil

Seasoning to taste (Lawry's Seasoned Salt, Morton's Nature's Seasons Seasoning Blend, garlic powder, ground pepper)

BACON AND CHEESE POTATOES

Like your taters with bacon and cheese? Prepare the potatoes as noted above, but add fresh bacon bits and sliced cheese during the last 20–30 minutes of cook time. Top with chives, and serve with sour cream. (The fresh garlic is optional but always delicious.)

Cooking with Cast Iron

Sauteed Asparagus

Not every dish needs to be steeped with bacon grease or fried to be delicious. In fact, Robby and I often enjoy a side of sautéed vegetables, using whatever is in season at the time. Growing up, my go-to veggies were squash and zucchini. I always thought asparagus was soft and bitter (like the stuff in the can) until Robby made it for me using the simple recipe below. By sautéing the asparagus in oil and spices, the acidity is removed, and the natural flavor is enhanced. This makes a delicious side to any beef, chicken, fish, or pasta dish.

Virtually any vegetable can be sautéed in a cast-iron skillet or grill. The key is to keep the heat low so you don't burn the food. With a low cooking temperature, you can also use light olive oil, which complements most veggies. And don't forget to season it to your taste and cook it until you're satisfied with the texture. (I prefer mine a little overdone by restaurant standards.)

The following recipe shows how easy it is to sauté veggies in cast iron. Once you've tried the asparagus, adapt the recipe to your favorites, from squash and zucchini to peppers and onions.

---

1. Place a small skillet over low-medium heat.

2. Add olive oil and asparagus to the pan. Season to taste. Turn periodically while cooking. The asparagus is done when it's the consistency you prefer.

½ Tbsp. olive oil

1 bundle fresh asparagus, cleaned with thick ends removed

Seasoning to taste (Morton's Nature's Seasons Seasoning Blend, ground pepper)

Modern Cast Iron

Shirley's Rice

When I was young, my grandmother would let me set the menu for my birthday dinner. It never crossed my mind to request pizza, hamburgers, or hot dogs. Instead, I wanted the good stuff—the home-cooked meals that were usually reserved for family gatherings. One of the sides I requested often was Shirley's rice. I never knew who Shirley was, but her rice continues to be legendary in my family for its rich aroma and robust flavor.

This recipe calls for chopped onion, celery, and bell pepper. To ensure the veggies are chopped fine enough, and to save time, I recommend using a food processor. (I picked mine up for about twenty dollars.) You can chop the veggies by hand if you need to, just make sure the pieces are small so they don't overwhelm the dish. When the rice is done, the veggies should be nearly invisible.

A small 2-quart Dutch oven is perfect for this dish, but you can use a bigger one or a deep-dish skillet.

---

1. Preheat oven to 350°F.

2. Place a small Dutch oven over medium heat. Add the butter, onion, celery, and bell pepper, and simmer until the onions are transparent. Add the mushrooms, consommé, and water and increase the heat to bring the mixture to a boil. Then add the rice and stir until combined.

3. Place the rice in the oven, and bake for 1 hour or until done.

¼ cup butter

½ small onion, chopped

1–2 stalks celery, chopped

1 green bell pepper, chopped

1 4-oz. can mushroom pieces, drained and chopped

1 10.5-oz. can beef consommé

½ cup water

1 cup white rice, uncooked

Papa's Sweet Potato Casserole

Every Thanksgiving, my grandfather contributes to the family meal by bringing a big sweet potato casserole. Topped with mini marshmallows, this sweet side has always been one of my favorites. When I realized how simple this dish is to make, I decided it should no longer be relegated to the holidays. While Papa's version is baked in a glass casserole dish, I found that cast iron heats it up nicely and keeps it warm longer.

   This recipe calls for a can of sweet potatoes, which is easy to keep on hand for a weeknight meal. We like Bruce's brand, but you can use whatever you prefer. Just be sure to use plain sweet potatoes, not pie filling. Oh and one other thing: don't forget the marshmallows!

---

1. Preheat oven to 400°F.

2. In a large bowl, mix the sugar and cinnamon into the sweet potatoes. Place the sweet potatoes in a large skillet, and bake for 15 minutes. Top the sweet potatoes with marshmallows, and broil until the marshmallows begin to melt. Be sure to watch the sweet potatoes while they broil so you don't burn the marshmallows.

3. Serve hot or cold. And don't be surprised if your family requests this for dessert.

½ Tbsp. brown sugar

1 tsp. cinnamon

1 29-oz. can baked sweet potatoes

1 bag mini marshmallows

Modern Cast Iron

Maduros

My mother used to live in Tampa, and it was there that she discovered a love for Cuban cooking, which she later instilled in us kids. My favorite Cuban side item is maduros, or fried sweet plantains. Plantains look like large bananas, but their orangeish flesh fries up to a sticky delicacy that has me craving them for dessert. While restaurants often deep-fry their maduros, I've found panfrying works just as well. When choosing your plantains, look for ones that are beginning to turn black and soften; they'll make the sweetest maduros.

This side is the perfect complement to Chicken & Yellow Rice. Find that recipe under Family Dinners in this chapter.

---

1. Place a skillet on low-medium heat.

2. Add oil and a single layer of plantains to the pan.

3. Heat the plantains about 5–10 minutes, turning occasionally. When the plantains are blackened on both sides, they're done—and now called maduros.

½ Tbsp. olive oil

1–2 ripe plantains, peeled and sliced diagonally into 1-inch pieces

Soups

Want to make something easy that's also hearty, inexpensive, and will give you plenty of leftovers? Then make a big pot of soup. Nothing goes so far with so little time and few ingredients—and it all cooks up in one pot!

In this section, I share family favorites from my mom and mother-in-law. All of the recipes make a large quantity of soup, so you'll want to use a sizable Dutch oven, about six quarts or larger. I like to use my enameled Dutch oven for these, but you can use bare cast iron, especially since the soups cook up rather quickly.

While hot soup is a great meal in the fall and winter, you don't have to wait for cold weather to enjoy them. The next time you have family or company over for dinner, take out your Dutch oven and make a meal worth sharing.

SAVE MONEY ON BEEF

Looking for ways to save money on your food budget? Most beef-based recipes—like the soups in this section—call for a pound of beef. However, you can often use as little as ½ or ¼ pound and still have a hearty meal, especially if you add more vegetables or potatoes.

You may also want to experiment with more budget-friendly meats like ground turkey or a mixture of ground beef and pork. And when you find ground beef on sale, stock up and freeze it in small batches in freezer bags. Just be sure to label the bags so you know what's in it and when you purchased it.

Beef & Vegetable Soup

When I was in school, I loved it when the lunchroom served beef and veggie soup because it was always accompanied by a PB&K sandwich—peanut butter mixed with light Karo syrup. To this day, I crave a PB&K every time I make beef and veggie soup.

In the following soup recipe, I recommend using a hearty vegetable mix that includes tomatoes, potatoes, carrots, green beans, lima beans, and okra. I like to add a little extra potato and carrot, as well. Although this is a beef soup, I prefer using chicken broth instead of beef broth, which gives it a milder flavor. If you're looking for something more robust, use beef broth instead.

1. Place a large Dutch oven over medium heat. Brown the ground beef with the onion and seasoning. Drain any excess grease and return to heat.

2. Add broth, tomato paste, vegetables, and Worcestershire sauce to the Dutch oven. Add water as desired. Let the ingredients simmer for 30 minutes or until the flavors are combined.

3. Serve hot (preferably with a PB&K sandwich).

1 lb. ground beef

1 large onion, chopped

Seasoning to taste (Lawry's Seasoned Salt, garlic powder)

1 14.5-oz. can chicken broth

1 6-oz. can tomato paste

1 15-oz. bag vegetable soup mix

1 potato, peeled and cubed

1–2 carrots, peeled and sliced

1 14.5-oz. can diced tomatoes

½ Tbsp. Worcestershire sauce

Mary Frances's Taco Soup

As soon as the temperature outside drops below 60 degrees, I make a big pot of taco soup using the following recipe from my mother-in-law. This soup is just as hearty as traditional chili, but it has a more robust flavor and is fun to eat piled high with shredded cheese, corn chips, and sour cream. Leftovers are even more flavorful the next night.

---

1. Place a large Dutch oven over medium heat. Add the ground beef and onion, along with half of the taco and ranch seasoning packets. Brown the beef, and drain any excess grease.

2. Add the remaining ingredients to the Dutch oven, including the rest of the taco and ranch seasoning packets. Add water to bring it to a desired consistency (somewhere between soup and chili). Let the ingredients simmer for 30 minutes or until the flavors are combined.

3. Serve with shredded cheese, corn chips (like Fritos), and sour cream.

1 lb. ground beef

1 large onion, chopped

1 packet taco seasoning mix

1 packet Hidden Valley's The Original Ranch Salad Dressing & Seasoning Mix

1 15.5-oz. can pinto beans

1 15-oz. can Ranch Style brand flavored pinto beans

1 15-oz. can whole-kernel corn

1 14.5-oz. can diced tomatoes

1 10-oz. can mild Ro*Tel Diced Tomatoes & Green Chilies

Shredded cheese, corn chips, and sour cream for serving

Bean & Sausage Soup

When I get a hankering for something other than chicken or beef, I reach in the freezer for a package of kielbasa. I like to keep this Polish sausage on hand because its mild flavor works well in so many dishes, especially this recipe for Bean & Sausage Soup.

While you can use any type or brand of sausage for this recipe, I prefer Hillshire Farm's Polska Kielbasa, which is fully cooked. I've used the beef, turkey, and regular polska (made with pork, turkey, and beef) varieties, and they all work well in this soup. However, I recommend the turkey sausage because it has the mildest flavor.

As for the beans, I like to use pinto and great northern beans, but navy or red beans would work well, too.

---

1. Place a large Dutch oven over medium heat. Sauté the kielbasa with the onion until done.

2. Add chicken broth, and use it to deglaze the Dutch oven.

3. Add the carrots, potatoes, beans, and seasoning, and enough water to reach the desired consistency. Let the soup simmer until carrots are soft, at least 30 minutes.

4. Add the kale, and simmer until tender, about 5 minutes.

5. Serve hot with Buttermilk Pour Biscuits.

1 14-oz. package polska kielbasa sausage, cut into 1-inch thick diagonal pieces

1 large onion, chopped

1 14.5-oz. can chicken broth

2 carrots, peeled and chopped

1–2 potatoes, diced

1 15.5-oz. can pinto beans, drained

1 15.5-oz. can great northern beans, drained

Seasoning to taste (Morton's Nature's Seasons Seasoning Blend, ground pepper)

3 leaves kale, torn into bite-size pieces

Cooking with Cast Iron

Sandwiches

Since I work from home, I usually eat a simple sandwich for lunch. When it's cold out, though, I prefer a hot meal. But who has time to cook on a lunch break?

The sandwiches in this section are a great compromise because they're filling, they're served hot, and they're quick and easy to make. They're also delicious, which is why it's not unusual for me to make these as an easy weeknight dinner.

Try the following two recipes, and then use your skillet to take your favorite sandwiches up a notch.

Grown-Up Grilled Ham & Cheese

A regular grilled cheese sandwich, made with just bread and cheese, can make a good side for a bowl of soup. However, this recipe for Grown-Up Grilled Ham & Cheese is hearty enough to serve by itself for lunch or dinner.

I've experimented with this simple recipe over the years, and while the ingredients can be changed to suit your taste, it's the cooking method that's key to the perfect grilled cheese. Instead of coating the bread with butter like most people recommend, put the butter in the pan and spread a thin layer of mayonnaise on the bread. The mayonnaise will spread more evenly and allow the bread to grill to a golden brown. Also, to ensure the cheese is properly melted, place a cookie sheet on the skillet while grilling. You could use a cast-iron or glass lid, but that would trap in moisture as well as heat, which would make the sandwich soggy. So pull out your cookie sheet for this recipe—just remember to use a pot holder because it'll get hot sitting on the skillet.

1. Place a small skillet on low heat.

2. Make a sandwich using all the ingredients listed above, making sure to spread a thin layer of mayonnaise on both the inside and outside of each piece of bread.

3. Melt a small pat of butter in the skillet. Place the sandwich in the skillet, and grill the bread until golden brown, flipping occasionally. Place a cookie sheet over the skillet while cooking to melt the cheese.

2 slices bread

Mayonnaise

Mustard

Cheddar or Colby-jack cheese, sliced

2 slices ham

3–5 dill pickle slices

1 pat butter

GRILLED ROAST BEEF SANDWICH WITH SMOKED CHEDDAR CHEESE

Make a sandwich using mayonnaise, mustard, roast beef, smoked cheddar cheese, tomato, and onion. Grill the sandwich as noted above.

Sloppy Joe

Sloppy joes are one of those meals we loved as children but forgot about as adults. I recently saw a packet of sloppy joe mix in the supermarket and developed a craving for it. (In my defense, I was seven months pregnant at the time and craving everything in sight.) Since I didn't want to pay more than two dollars for the little seasoning packet, I went home and made my own version from scratch. It was so good, and so much healthier than the store-bought stuff, that I added it to our family's weeknight menu. With a recipe this simple, you'll enjoy bringing back this childhood fave.

1. Place a large skillet over medium heat. Brown the ground beef with the onion and a few shakes of Lawry's Seasoned Salt. Drain any excess grease, and return to heat.

2. In a bowl, mix together the tomato sauce, vinegar, sugar, and remaining seasonings. Taste the mixture and add more seasoning as desired. Add the sauce to the meat, and lightly simmer until it cooks down.

3. Spread butter on the buns, and toast them in a toaster oven or in a separate skillet. Spread mayonnaise on the toasted buns, and top with the Sloppy Joe mixture. Serve hot with a fork and extra napkins.

1 lb. ground beef

1 small onion, chopped

Seasoning to taste
(Lawry's Seasoned Salt)

1 8-oz. can tomato sauce

1 ½ Tbsp. white distilled vinegar

½ Tbsp. sugar

¼ tsp. each garlic powder, paprika, chili powder, onion powder

Hamburger buns

1 pat butter

Mayonnaise to taste

Weeknight Meals

Whether you're a stay-at-home mom or a business professional, weeknights are always busy. No matter how much prep work you do on the weekends, it seems there's never enough time to prepare a homemade meal. But before you order pizza (again!), try one of the following recipes. They're sized just right for two people, and most of the ingredients can be stored in the pantry, fridge, or freezer for when you need them. Even better, all of these meals can be made in about 30 minutes.

COLESLAW

Sweet coleslaw makes a cool side item for hot fried foods like Crispy Coconut Chicken Tenders or Salmon Cakes. And since it's made with cabbage and carrots, you can use your leftover veggies from the Cabbage Boil.

1. Place the shredded cabbage and carrot in a large bowl.

2. In a separate bowl, mix together mayonnaise, vinegar, and sugar. Adjust the ingredients to taste. (You want it to be sweet with a slight tang.) Stir in the salt and pepper.

3. Add the mayonnaise mixture to the shredded cabbage and carrot, and mix well.

4. Serve immediately or cool in the refrigerator first.

¼–½ head of cabbage, shredded

1 carrot, peeled and shredded

3–4 Tbsp. mayonnaise

1–2 Tbsp. white distilled vinegar

1–2 Tbsp. sugar

Salt and freshly-ground pepper to taste

Crispy Coconut Chicken Tenders

This dish is a bit funky, but if you're into healthy alternatives (especially gluten-free ones), you just might like these crispy-but-not-fried chicken tenders. That crispy coating comes from shredded coconut. Although it's unsweetened, it does add a tropical flair to the chicken. Feel free to temper that with seasonings like sea salt, pepper, and garlic powder. I like to dip mine in mild BBQ sauce.

To make, choose a skillet or grill large enough to hold the chicken tenders without overlapping. I suggest adding a bit of cooking oil to keep the chicken from sticking, but don't overdo it; this dish is baked, not fried.

---

1. Preheat oven to 375°F. Use paper towels to oil the skillet.

2. Place the flour, eggs, and coconut in three separate bowls. Season the chicken tenders, and dip them in the flour, eggs, and coconut (in that order). Press the coconut into the chicken to create a nice coating.

3. Place chicken in the skillet, and bake for 16 minutes, turning halfway through the cook time. Then broil the chicken for 3–5 minutes or until the coconut coating is evenly browned. (Be careful not to burn the coconut.) Serve with your favorite dip and a side of Coleslaw.

½ Tbsp. olive oil (for the pan)

¼ cup all-purpose flour

2 eggs, whisked together

1 cup shredded, unsweetened coconut

1 lb. chicken tenders

Seasoning to taste (Nature's Seasons blend, ground pepper, garlic powder)

BAKED CHICKEN TENDERS
Not into coconut? Use panko or seasoned bread crumbs instead. You could even add some shredded Parmesan if you're feeling a bit cheesy.

Stay-at-Home Steak

Steakhouses often advertise the biggest, thickest steaks, but in our house, we prefer the simple rib eye. It's usually more tender and flavorful than other cuts, and its thinner size makes it easier to cook at home. Still, there's a knack to cooking steak: it's all about the sear. In this recipe, I explain how to sear the steak and then finish cooking it in the oven. If your steak is thin, or you prefer it rare, you can avoid baking it by simply searing it for a longer time on the stove. Either way, the next time you're craving a juicy steak, stay at home and make one for less than half the price those restaurants charge.

For this recipe, a regular skillet works fine, but if you have a grill pan, use it to create those mouthwatering, seared-in grill lines. Since you'll be using a higher temperature to sear the steak, use avocado oil or another oil with a high smoke point. For a richer steak, top with a pat of butter while cooking.

1. Preheat oven to 450°F.

2. Let the steaks rest on the counter for several minutes until they reach room temperature.

3. Place a skillet over medium-high heat.

4. Blot the steaks with a paper towel to absorb excess moisture, and then season the meat. Add oil to the skillet. Flick a few drops of water into the skillet; if it sizzles and evaporates, the oil is hot enough. Add the steaks to the hot pan, and let them cook uninterrupted for 2 minutes. Flip the steaks to sear the other side for 2 minutes. The steaks will stick to the pan a bit while they sear and will release when browned.

5. Place the skillet in the oven, and bake for about 10 minutes or until the steaks are as done as you like. (For medium, a meat thermometer should register 145°F.) Remove the steaks and let them rest on a plate for 10 minutes to finish cooking. During this time, the temperature will rise another 5 degrees, and the juices will settle back into the meat. Avoid cutting the steaks until the 10 minutes is over.

6. Serve hot, preferably with Garlic Potatoes and Sautéed Asparagus.

2 thin rib eye steaks

Coarse salt and freshly ground pepper to taste

¼–½ Tbsp. avocado oil

Fajitas

Love Mexican night? Switch it up by substituting those tacos with steaming fajitas.

Flank steak is traditionally used in fajitas, but it tends to be tough (which is why it's usually marinated). Instead, a thin rib eye steak with a good marbling of fat will make the most tender fajitas you've ever had. You can even use leftover steak and reheat it in a hot skillet (not the microwave, or it'll get tough).

There are lots of seasoning options in your local supermarket, from seasoning packets to sauce mixes, most of which feature cumin and chili powder. Though normally used in Italian dishes, a dash of oregano will make the other flavors stand out. I also like to use Worcestershire sauce, which adds a richness to the meat.

A lot of fajitas recipes will have you cook the steak whole and then slice it, but I like to slice it first and then cook it. Since the pieces are smaller, the steak cooks up faster, and I know it's cooked thoroughly. Meat and vegetables cook at different rates, so I recommend cooking them separately.

This entire meal can be prepared using two skillets, but you could use a griddle for the steak or a grill pan for the tortillas. Fajitas are usually prepared with flour tortillas, but I use soft corn tortillas instead (which taste just as good!).

Serve the steak, peppers, and tortillas in the hot skillets and let everyone make their own fajitas at the table. This keeps the ingredients warm and makes dinner a fun make-your-own experience.

---

1. Let the steak pieces rest on the counter for several minutes until they reach room temperature.

2. Place a skillet over medium heat.

3. Blot the steak pieces with a paper towel to absorb excess moisture and then season the meat with salt and pepper. Add oil to the skillet and brown the steak. Then add the fajita seasoning and cook for 3–4 minutes.

1 thin rib eye steak, cut into long, thin pieces

Salt and freshly ground pepper to taste

1 Tbsp. olive oil

1 fajita seasoning packet (or a mixture of cumin, chili powder, and oregano)

1 sweet onion, chopped

4. Remove the steak and sauté the onions, bell peppers, and jalapeño peppers in the same skillet. When they soften a bit and peppers develop brown spots, they're done.

5. Place the steak back in the skillet with the peppers, and add the Worcestershire sauce. Reduce heat and cook for 2–3 minutes.

6. Warm the tortillas in a separate skillet.

7. Serve hot in the skillets with sides of lime slices, cilantro, sour cream, and salsa.

1 green bell pepper, sliced

1 yellow bell pepper, sliced

1 orange bell pepper, sliced

2 jalapeño peppers (optional)

½ Tbsp. Worcestershire sauce

1 package soft tortillas (flour or corn)

Lime slices, cilantro, sour cream, and salsa for serving

SAUCY FAJITAS

Even tasty fajitas can turn out dry. Combat this by making a light sauce for the steak.

1. Use the recipe for Fajitas. After cooking the steak and peppers, remove them from the skillet and add ½ Tbsp. Worcestershire sauce, 1–2 Tbsp. water, ¼ cup beef broth, and 1 tsp. corn starch to thicken it a bit.

2. Let simmer for 3–5 minutes, then add the meat and peppers back to the skillet. Reduce heat and cook for 2–3 minutes before serving.

Beef Stroganoff

Beef Stroganoff is a simple, satisfying meal that makes a pound of beef go a long way. Stew beef is typically used, but that cut of meat can be quite tough. Instead, I prefer a chuck roast cut into 2-inch cubes.

You can prepare this dish in a large skillet or Dutch oven. You'll also need a pot to boil the noodles. And if you'd like to try a different kind of pasta, go for it. I've found that gluten-free spirals work just as well as egg noodles.

_____

1. Let the steak pieces rest on the counter for several minutes until they reach room temperature.

2. Boil noodles in a pot.

3. Place a large skillet over medium heat and add oil.

4. Blot the steak pieces with a paper towel to absorb excess moisture. Season the meat, and then coat it with flour. Add the steak pieces to the hot skillet and cook thoroughly, flipping periodically. Once cooked, remove the steak from the pan.

5. Add onions and mushrooms to the hot pan and simmer until the onions are transparent. Add the beef consommé, and use it to deglaze the pan. Add the cream of mushroom soup and the cooked steak pieces.

6. Add the cooked noodles to the skillet. Stir all ingredients until combined and simmer 5 minutes.

1 lb. chuck roast cut into 2-inch cubes

1 12-oz. package egg noodles

2 Tbsp. olive oil

Seasoning to taste (Lawry's Seasoned Salt, ground pepper)

2 Tbsp. all-purpose flour

1 sweet onion, chopped

1 4-oz. can mushroom pieces, drained and chopped

1 10.5-oz. can beef consommé

1 10.5-oz. can condensed cream of mushroom soup

GROUND BEEF STROGANOFF

Instead of using (and paying for) steak, make the Beef Stroganoff recipe using a pound of ground beef. It's like a healthier, homemade version of Hamburger Helper.

Cooking with Cast Iron

Alfredo Sauce

I never liked Alfredo dishes until my mother gave me her recipe for Alfredo sauce. Made with real cream and Parmesan cheese—not the fake stuff found in the bottle—this sauce makes a decadent meal when paired with your favorite meat and pasta.

The flavor of this sauce relies on the heavy cream and Parmesan cheese (definitely not diet-friendly fare!). A pinch of chili powder enhances the flavor, but don't overdo it. Since this is a creamy sauce, you'll need to stir it continuously while cooking, so have all your ingredients prepared and ready to add to the pan.

---

1. Place a small skillet on low-medium heat, and melt the butter. Pour cream in the skillet, and add the salt. Heat the cream for 2–3 minutes while stirring.

2. Add the cheese slowly while stirring to keep it from clumping together. Continue to cook while stirring for 3–5 minutes or until Alfredo sauce reaches the desired consistency. Stir in the chili powder.

3. Pour the Alfredo sauce over your favorite pasta.

2 Tbsp. butter

1 16-oz. carton heavy whipping cream

Pinch of salt

½ cup fresh Parmesan cheese, shredded or grated

Pinch of chili powder

CREAMED SPINACH

Looking for ways to increase your veggie intake? Make some creamed spinach everyone will enjoy. Simply prepare a skillet of homemade Alfredo Sauce, then add a 10-oz. box of frozen spinach, remembering to thaw and drain the spinach before adding it to the skillet. Simmer until done, then top with extra Parmesan cheese.

SAUSAGE ALFREDO

The homemade Alfredo Sauce makes this dish nice and creamy, while the capers give it a robust flavor. I make this a lot with polska or turkey kielbasa, but you can use other meats such as grilled chicken, shrimp, or scallops. As for the pasta, I prefer rotini or penne, but you can use whatever you have on hand.

_____

1. Boil pasta in a pot.

2. Place a large skillet on medium-high heat. Brown the sausage, then remove it from the pan. Reduce heat and make homemade Alfredo Sauce in the same skillet. Deglaze the pan with a spatula. Add the capers, including some of the juice from the jar.

3. Add the cooked sausage and pasta to the skillet, combining all the ingredients. Stir in the tomatoes, and top with extra Parmesan cheese.

1 package pasta

1 14-oz. package polska kielbasa sausage, cut diagonally into 1-inch pieces

Homemade Alfredo Sauce

2 Tbsp. capers

1 small tomato, diced

½ Tbsp. Parmesan cheese

Salmon with Artichokes

I usually don't eat seafood at home because I don't like to smell it cooking. The exception to that rule is salmon because it doesn't have the same fishy smell as other seafood. Plus, I can make a delicious salmon dinner for a quarter of what I would pay in a restaurant.

This recipe for pan-seared salmon with artichokes and capers is truly delicious. You can certainly use fresh salmon for this, but I buy packs of frozen, individually sealed fillets from the grocery store, which allows me to keep a few on hand for quick weeknight meals. The fillets can be defrosted in about five minutes in a bowl of warm water, and the entire dish takes only about ten minutes to cook. You can't beat that!

Always select wild caught, Alaskan salmon, which has less mercury than farmed salmon. The artichokes and capers add a robust, earthy flavor, while the lemon juice cuts the fishiness. If you're not familiar with artichokes and capers, they can usually be found on the same aisle as pickles, and they last a long time in the fridge once they're opened. Artichokes are fibrous, so I recommend using a pair of kitchen scissors to cut them into smaller pieces. To maximize the flavor of the capers, include some of the liquid from the jar.

Salmon is often served rare, but I prefer it cooked to medium. For that reason, this recipe calls for pan-searing the bottom (skin-side) of the salmon and then baking it until it's done. If you prefer your salmon rare, you may just want to pan-sear the bottom and skip the oven. However, if you like it a bit crispy, you could pan-sear both sides. Experiment to see how you like it best.

_____

1. Preheat oven to 350°F.

2. Place a skillet over medium heat and add the ghee. Place the salmon in the skillet skin-side down (if the skin is still intact) and season it. Sear the salmon for 3–4 minutes and turn off the heat. Add artichokes and capers and sprinkle with fresh lemon juice.

3. Bake the salmon for 7 minutes or until done. Serve hot with a side of Sautéed Asparagus or on a bed of salad or pasta.

½ Tbsp. ghee or oil

2 salmon fillets

Seasoning to taste (Morton's Nature's Seasons Seasoning Blend, ground pepper)

¼ cup artichoke pieces

2 Tbsp. capers

1 tsp. fresh lemon juice

Salmon Cakes

A tasty twist on traditional crab cakes, salmon cakes are easy and economical to make. Although you can serve them as appetizers, I like to make them as a special treat for lunch.

If you have leftover salmon, use it to make your salmon cakes. If not, choose high-quality canned Alaskan salmon. Also, take the time to sauté the onion, as this adds a sweetness to the salmon cakes. If you want a more zesty flavor, use Italian bread crumbs.

1. Place a small skillet over medium heat. Add 1–2 teaspoons of oil to the pan and sauté the onions until they're transparent. Remove the pan from the heat and place the onions in a large bowl.

2. Add the egg to the onions and whisk together. Add the salmon, using a fork to break up any large pieces. Add half the bread crumbs, lemon juice, and seasoning, combining all ingredients together. Slowly add more bread crumbs until the mixture is firm enough to form 4 or 5 patties the size of the palm of your hand.

3. Reheat the skillet on medium-high and add enough oil to cover the bottom and sides of the salmon cakes. Add the salmon cakes to the skillet, and panfry, flipping the cakes over when the bottoms are golden brown.

4. Serve with a bottle of Crystal brand hot sauce and a side of Coleslaw.

¼–1 cup avocado oil (or another oil with a high smoke point)

1 small onion, chopped

1 egg

1 7.5-oz. can cooked salmon

¾ cup bread crumbs

1 tsp. lemon juice

Seasoning to taste (Morton's Nature's Seasons Seasoning Blend, ground pepper, garlic powder)

Crystal brand hot sauce for serving

-169-

Cooking with Cast Iron

Eggplant Parmesan

I love the flavor of eggplant Parmesan, but I never order it in restaurants. That's because most restaurants cut the eggplant into thick pieces, resulting in a soggy dish. To me, the key to perfect eggplant Parm is to slice the eggplant thin (about half an inch) and panfry each piece to a crisp before topping it with the marinara sauce and cheese and baking it. A large cast-iron skillet is ideal for this, but you can also use a grill or griddle.

1. Preheat oven to 400°F. Place a large skillet over medium-high heat and add the oil.

2. Place egg whites and bread crumbs in separate bowls. Season each slice of eggplant on both sides. Dip the eggplant in the egg whites and then the bread crumbs.

3. Place the eggplant slices in the hot skillet and panfry for 3–4 minutes or until the bottoms are golden brown.

4. Flip the eggplant over, and spoon a dollop of marinara sauce onto each slice. Be careful not to pour the sauce into the skillet or it will burn. Top each slice with Parmesan cheese.

5. Place the skillet in the oven, and bake for 5–7 minutes or until cheese is melted. Serve hot with pasta.

1–2 Tbsp. avocado oil (or another oil with a high smoke point)

2 egg whites

¾ cup bread crumbs

1 large eggplant, sliced into medallions ½-inch thick

Seasoning to taste (Italian seasoning, salt)

1 jar marinara sauce

Parmesan cheese, shredded

Family Dinners

Cooking for the whole family shouldn't take the whole day or cost a whole paycheck. In this section, I provide several recipes that feed four or more people but take less than an hour to prepare and cook, all the while using ingredients that are simple and inexpensive. Whether you're cooking for small kids or elderly parents, everyone will agree these dishes are nothing short of good ol' fashioned comfort food.

So get cooking, and then get comfortable around the table.

Southern Fried Chicken

I still remember Great-Grandma serving delicious homemade fried chicken at a family get-together, even though I couldn't have been more than three years old at the time. My grandmother, who was a wonderful cook, tried the same recipe, but her fried chicken never turned out as crispy as Great-Grandma's.

If you talk to folks about fried chicken, you'll hear two things: it's a true Southern delicacy worthy of the finest restaurant, and it takes a special talent to get it right. Unfortunately, I lack that talent. I've tried—trust me, I've tried—but I just can't fry chicken like Great-Grandma did.

And while I'm being really honest here, it scares me a bit to handle a large skillet or Dutch oven full of hot oil. I also don't like the idea of using—and consuming—so much grease.

Nevertheless, this is a book about cast iron, and it wouldn't be complete without a recipe for traditional Southern Fried Chicken. I hope you can use it to develop a talent that will wow your family for generations.

To start with, you'll need to purchase a pound or more of lard (pork fat). You can still get this at most supermarkets next to the vegetable shortening. You'll also need some buttermilk—not regular (or "sweet") milk, which doesn't have the same acidity or flavor. I recommend using chicken legs and thighs since they're smaller than breasts and easier to cook thoroughly.

As for frying the chicken, you'll need a deep skillet or Dutch oven large enough to hold the chicken and the oil it's immersed in with at least a couple inches to spare. To reduce the amount of oil needed, you can use a smaller skillet or Dutch oven, though you may need to fry the chicken in batches.

You'll also need a couple accessories, including a cooking thermometer that clasps onto the side of the skillet or Dutch oven, and a sturdy pair of tongs. If you have a fry basket and splatter screen, use those as well.

Good luck!

1. Clip a cooking thermometer on the inside of the deep skillet. Heat the skillet on medium-high and add the lard. Adjust the cooking temperature until the lard stabilizes between 350–375°F.

2. Place the buttermilk and flour in separate bowls. Season the chicken, then dip each piece in the buttermilk and then in the flour.

3. Using metal tongs, carefully place each piece of chicken in the skillet, and fry until done. (A meat thermometer should register 175°F.) After placing the chicken in the skillet, you may need to add more lard to cover the chicken completely. You may also need to adjust the heat to keep the lard at the right temperature.

Lard (enough to completely cover the chicken)

2 cups buttermilk

2 cups all-purpose flour

Salt and freshly-ground pepper to taste

1–2 lb. chicken legs and/or thighs (with the bone and skin intact)

4. Once the chicken is cooked thoroughly, use the tongs to place each piece on a cookie sheet lined with paper towels to drain the excess oil.

5. Serve hot or cold, and don't forget the biscuits.

PANFRIED CHICKEN

One of the hardest parts about frying chicken is cooking the meat thoroughly while keeping the coating from burning. In this variation of the traditional recipe, you'll crisp the outside of the chicken by panfrying it one side at a time, and then finish cooking it in the oven. You'll still get the crispy fried chicken you know and love, but you'll be sure it's cooked all the way through—and you'll use less oil in the process. When I want fried chicken, this is how I make it.

_____

1. Preheat oven to 400°F.

2. Prepare the chicken as noted in the Southern Fried Chicken recipe. Heat the skillet and add lard until it measures about ¾ inch deep (enough to cover the bottom and sides of the chicken). Place the chicken in the skillet. (If you're cooking a chicken breast or thigh, place it in the skillet skin-side down.) Add more lard to the skillet if necessary, and adjust the heat as needed to keep the lard between 350–375°F. Fry until golden brown, about 6 minutes, flipping halfway through.

3. Once the coating is crispy, you can place the chicken in the oven to finish cooking. However, you don't want to bake the chicken in the pan because it has a lot of grease in it, and that would make the chicken soggy. Instead of removing the chicken, pouring out the hot grease, and then returning the chicken to the pan, simply place the chicken on a cookie sheet. Then bake until the chicken is done, about 12–18 minutes. If you have a wire rack that fits in your cookie sheet, use it to promote air circulation and avoid burn spots.

Modern Cast Iron

Baked Chicken

There are a lot of baked chicken recipes out there, but most of them result in chicken that's either too rubbery or too bland. This recipe from my Aunt Sandie is totally different. By searing the chicken skin-side down before baking it, you create a crispy coating and lock in the juices and flavors. I recommend using legs or thighs for this recipe because they cook up faster than breasts and tend to have more flavor.

Remember that you're baking the chicken, though, not frying it. That's why only a tablespoon or less of vegetable shortening is needed. As soon as the skin is crispy, flip the chicken over and place it in the oven to finish cooking.

1. Preheat oven to 400°F.

2. Place a large skillet on medium heat, and add the vegetable shortening.

3. Season the chicken and place each piece in the skillet. For chicken thighs, place them skin side down. Sear the chicken until crispy, about 3–5 minutes. Turn the chicken pieces over, and turn off the heat.

4. Bake for 30–45 minutes or until done. (A meat thermometer should register 175°F.)

5. Serve hot, preferably with a side of Collard Greens.

1 Tbsp. vegetable shortening

1 lb. chicken legs and/or thighs (with the bone and skin intact)

Seasoning to taste (Lawry's Seasoned Salt, ground pepper, garlic powder)

Chicken & Yellow Rice

Chicken and rice is a staple no matter what part of the country you live in, but in our family, we prefer it made with yellow rice. This mouth-watering rice gets its color and flavor from the spice saffron. Variations of this dish are common in Spanish and Cuban cuisine, which heavily influence our palate here in Florida.

    This recipe calls for a rotisserie chicken, but you can certainly use leftover meat from the Baked Chicken dish. We prefer Vigo Yellow Rice, but any brand of saffron yellow rice should do.

---

1. Place a large Dutch oven over medium heat. Prepare a packet of rice, following the directions on the bag. For extra flavor, substitute a cup of water with 1 ¼ cups of chicken broth.

2. Once the rice is cooked, stir in the chicken and reduce heat to low. Cook for 12–15 minutes, stirring periodically.

3. Serve topped with black beans and a side of Maduros.

1 10-oz. package of Vigo Yellow Rice

1 ¼ cups chicken broth (optional)

1 rotisserie chicken, deboned

1 15-oz. can black beans for serving

Mom's Chicken Pot Pie

One of my all-time favorite meals is Mom's Chicken Pot Pie. Rich and creamy with a crispy crust, this dish has everything.

 This recipe makes a large pot pie, but it's topped with a 9-inch pie crust. A small Dutch oven works well, but you could us a larger Dutch oven or a deep skillet. Another option is to make two chicken pot pies using 9-inch skillets. Just remember to buy more pie crusts if you use a larger pan or multiple pans.

 This recipe calls for four types of canned condensed soups, but only a few tablespoons are needed of the potato and chicken and herb soups. I recommend freezing the excess in ice cube trays, then transferring the cubes to freezer bags for later use. (Trust me, you'll want to make this again real soon.)

----

1. Preheat oven to 400°F.

2. Use paper towels to oil the inside of a Dutch oven.

3. Place the soups, creams, and vegetables in a large bowl. Mix in the chicken pieces, and season to taste. If the mixture appears too thick, stir in some of the chicken broth.

4. Line the bottom of the Dutch oven with a pie crust. Add the chicken mixture, and top with the second pie crust. Bake for 40–50 minutes or until crust is golden brown.

½ Tbsp. oil (for Dutch oven)

1 10.5-oz. can condensed cream of mushroom soup

1 10.5-oz. can condensed cream of chicken soup

3 Tbsp. condensed chicken and herb soup

4 Tbsp. condensed cream of potato soup

¼ cup cream

1 dollop sour cream

1 cup frozen mixed vegetables including peas, carrots, and corn (defrosted)

1 rotisserie chicken, deboned

Seasoning to taste (Morton's Nature's Seasons Seasoning blend, ground pepper, garlic powder)

¼–½ cup chicken broth (optional)

2 frozen deep-dish pie crusts (defrosted)

EASIEST CHICKEN POT PIE

If you're running low on ingredients or time, try this super-simple version of chicken pot pie.

---

1. Preheat oven to 350 degrees F.

2. Use paper towels to oil the inside of a Dutch oven.

3. Mix soup and vegetables in a bowl, and add in chicken pieces and season to taste. Place in the Dutch oven and bake for 15 minutes or until ingredients begin to bubble. Place biscuit dough on top, and bake for an additional 13–17 minutes or until biscuits are golden brown.

1 10.5-oz. can cream of chicken soup

1 cup frozen mixed vegetables including peas, carrots, and corn (defrosted)

1 rotisserie chicken, deboned

Seasoning to taste (Morton's Nature's Seasons Seasoning blend, ground pepper, garlic powder)

1 16-oz. can refrigerated biscuits

Beef Pot Roast

I used to think the only way to make a good pot roast was to cook it for hours in a Crock-Pot. However, cooking meat low and slow can make it tough and flavorless. On the other hand, Dutch ovens are ideal for cooking pot roasts because their heavy lids trap in moisture and heat, leaving the meat tender and juicy. As a bonus, a roast prepared in a Dutch oven can be cooked in less than half the time of one cooked in a Crock-Pot (just don't leave the oven unattended).

In the following recipe, I recommend using a large Dutch oven to first brown the meat and then bake it until done. By using the same Dutch oven for both browning and baking, you'll be able to make the most of the meat drippings, maximizing the flavor of the dish. Adding the vegetables partway through the cooking time will help you avoid soggy veggies. And the flavor? Well, this is the best pot roast I've ever had. I think you'll agree.

1. Preheat oven to 375°F.

2. Let the roast rest on the counter for several minutes until it reaches room temperature.

3. Place a large Dutch oven over medium-high heat and add oil.

4. Blot the roast with a paper towel to absorb excess moisture, and then season the meat.

5. Once the oil is hot enough, sear the meat on both sides until brown. Reduce the heat and add the chicken broth. Deglaze the Dutch oven using a spatula and then add half the onions. Place a lid on the Dutch oven and bake for 1 ½ hours.

2 lb. chuck roast

½ Tbsp. avocado oil (or another oil with a high smoke point)

Seasoning to taste (Lawry's Seasoned Salt, Cavender's All Purpose Greek Seasoning, ground pepper)

1 14.5-oz. can chicken broth

1 sweet onion, sliced

3–4 cups water

4 carrots, peeled and cut to 1-inch pieces

3 large russet potatoes, peeled and cut to 1-inch pieces

6. Reduce heat to 350°F. Add 3–4 cups of water to keep the roast moist and bake an additional hour. Then add the rest of the onions, carrots, potatoes, and more water (if needed), and bake an additional 45 minutes to an hour or until meat is tender and veggies are soft.

7. Serve with hot Mayonnaise Biscuits.

CREAMY POT ROAST

My mother-in-law makes a delicious pot roast with the veggies on the side. Here's how.

1. Start with the recipe for Beef Pot Roast.

2. Season the meat with Lawry's Seasoned Salt, ground pepper, and a quarter of a pack of Lipton Recipe Secrets Onion Recipe Soup & Dip Mix.

3. Mix a 10.5-oz. can of condensed cream of mushroom soup with the rest of the onion mix, and use it in place of the veggies.

4. Sear and bake the roast as noted above.

Meatloaf

With little more than a pound of ground beef, you can make a tasty meatloaf for the whole family. Leftovers can be turned into meatloaf sandwiches the next day or frozen for another night.

 Many recipes call for bread crumbs, but that tends to produce a drier meatloaf. Instead, I recommend starting with two slices of bread dipped in milk. If the meat mixture is too runny to bind together well, you can then add bread crumbs until you're able to form a solid meatloaf.

 Meatloaf undoubtedly gets its humble name from the fact that it's a baked loaf of meat. You can create that loaf shape by pressing the meat into a cast-iron loaf pan. However, since the meat touches the sides of the pan, only the top of the loaf will brown. Instead, I suggest using your hands to mold the meat into a loaf shape and then placing it in a large cast-iron skillet, leaving at least a half an inch in between the meat and the sides of the pan for air to circulate. This will allow both the top and the sides of the loaf to brown nicely.

---

1. Preheat oven to 360°F.

2. Rub oil into a large skillet.

3. Place the ground beef in a large bowl and mix in the onion, sauces, eggs, and half of the ketchup. Stir in the seasoning.

4. In a separate bowl, place the bread pieces in the milk, allowing them to soak up the liquid. Add the bread to the meat mixture and combine well. Using your hands, mold the meat into the shape of a loaf and place it in the skillet. If the mixture is too

½ Tbsp. oil (for the pan)

1 lb. ground beef

1 sweet onion, chopped

3 Tbsp. BBQ sauce

½ Tbsp. Worcestershire sauce

2 eggs, whisked together

⅓ cup ketchup

soft to form a loaf, slowly add the bread crumbs until the
consistency is firm enough.

5. Bake for 30 minutes. Remove the skillet from the oven, and
   top the meatloaf with remaining ketchup. Continue baking
   for 15–30 minutes or until done.

Seasoning to taste
(Lawry's Seasoned Salt,
Morton's Nature's Seasons
Seasoning Blend, ground
pepper)

2 slices white bread, torn
into small pieces

¼ cup milk

¼–½ cup bread crumbs

MINI MEATLOAVES

Instead of one big meatloaf, you can make several Mini
Meatloaves, which are more fun to eat and are easier to freeze and
reheat later.

To make, use the Meatloaf recipe but form smaller loaves the
size of the palm of your hand. Place these in multiple skillets or
on a long grill or griddle so that they're not touching each other.
Bake as directed above, but keep an eye on the meatloaves to avoid
burning. The overall cooking time will be a few minutes less than
with a single large meatloaf.

Shepherd's Pie

Looking for comfort food that you can make for the whole family on a busy weeknight? This recipe for Shepherd's Pie is made even easier by using premade mashed potatoes. You can use dehydrated or refrigerated mashed potatoes, but I prefer the frozen medallions at Trader Joe's; they're the closest thing I've found to the real thing but with less sodium than other premade potatoes.

Whether you make your potatoes from scratch or get a little help, this dish will have you reaching for seconds.

---

1. Preheat oven to 400°F.

2. Place a large skillet over medium heat. Brown the ground beef with the onion, seasoning, Better than Bouillon Beef Base, and Worcestershire sauce. Drain off any excess grease.

3. Layer the mixed vegetables on top of the beef, followed by a layer of the mashed potatoes. Top with the cheddar cheese. Bake for 30–40 minutes.

TATER TOT SHEPHERD'S PIE

Start with the Shepherd's Pie recipe but, instead of mashed potatoes, use frozen tater tots. Their crispy texture and light seasoning gives a fun but tasty twist to this grown-up dish.

1 lb. ground beef

1 small onion, chopped

Seasoning to taste (Lawry's Seasoned Salt, ground pepper)

½ Tbsp. Better than Bouillon Beef Base

½ Tbsp. Worcestershire sauce

⅔ cup frozen mixed vegetables including peas, carrots, and corn (defrosted)

3–4 cups prepared mashed potatoes

½ cup cheddar cheese, shredded

Sausage & Cabbage

Not a fan of bitter cabbage? Me either. But in this dish, mild kielbasa, potatoes, and carrots work together to bring out the natural sweetness of the cabbage. Trust me, this dish is worth trying.

In this recipe, I recommend browning the sausage first so you can deglaze the pot and use the drippings to season the cabbage. However, you don't want to boil or steam the sausage after it's browned, so you'll need to remove the sausage and then add it back after the cabbage has cooked down. This extra step will give you the best texture and flavor. While it doesn't take long to prep or cook this dish, it does make a lot of servings, so it's perfect for a family dinner.

---

1. Place a large Dutch oven on medium heat and add the bacon grease. Brown the sausage and then remove it from the Dutch oven.

2. Add ½ cup of water and use it to deglaze the Dutch oven. Add the cabbage and carrots and enough water to cover the bottom of the pot. Cover and cook for 15 minutes.

3. Add the potatoes, browned sausage, and seasoning. Replace the lid and continue cooking until done, about 20 minutes.

4. Serve hot with Mayonnaise Biscuits.

2 Tbsp. bacon grease

1 14-oz. package polska kielbasa sausage, cut diagonally into 1-inch pieces

3 cups room-temperature water, divided

1 head cabbage, cut into bite-sized pieces

2 large carrots, peeled and sliced

2 russet potatoes, peeled and cubed

Seasoning to taste (Morton's Nature's Seasons Seasoning Blend, ground pepper, garlic powder)

Cooking with Cast Iron

Desserts

You've seen how to make an entire dinner in cast iron. But what about dessert?

It may surprise you, but the same qualities that make cast iron the perfect baking pan for cornbread also make it ideal for cobblers, pies, crisps, brownies, and cookies. You can even bake a cake in cast-iron loaf pans or fluted pans. The cast iron's ability to retain and transfer heat ensures these desserts are baked evenly and, if desired, have a nice crispy edge.

There are plenty of cast-iron pans available to help you make the dessert of your dreams, but all of the recipes in this section can be baked in small (8- or 9-inch) or large (10- or 12-inch) skillets. One thing to keep in mind when baking in cast iron is that you can't store leftovers in the pan. So if you can't eat that last slice of Skillet Cookie Cake, be sure to store it in something else. You may even want to freeze it in a freezer-safe bag for the next time you get a cookie craving.

FREEZING BLUEBERRIES

I never know when I'm going to crave blueberry cobbler or want to make a compote for breakfast, so I keep a few cups of blueberries in the freezer at all times. Fortunately, we have blueberry bushes in our yard, so I stock up every summer (for free!).

You can stock up on berries, too, if you buy them in season at your local farmer's market. Don't just stick them in the freezer, though, or they'll freeze into one hard lump. Instead, rinse them in a colander and lay them out on a cookie sheet lined with paper towels to dry. Then remove the paper towels and place the cookie sheet in the freezer. This will allow each berry to freeze individually. The next day, transfer the berries to freezer-safe bags and place them back in the freezer for those early-morning baking emergencies.

BAKING WITH FLOUR

Flour is such a common ingredient in most desserts that it deserves special mention, especially if you're like me and most of your baking experience involves opening a box of Duncan Hines.

When baking, you need to make sure you're using the right kind of flour, whether it's all-purpose or self-rising. (If it doesn't say self-rising on the bag, then assume it's not.)

As its name implies, all-purpose flour can be used to cook everything from gravy to brownies. However, when baking desserts that are supposed to rise—like cakes—you'll need some help to leaven it or fluff it up. Some recipes call for self-rising flour, which contains baking powder and salt in just the right amounts to make the dessert rise (without you needing to add yeast). Other recipes call for all-purpose flour, but then have you add the leavening ingredients separately. In either case, just follow the recipe as written, and it'll turn out fine.

It's a good idea to keep both all-purpose and self-rising flour on hand. If you run out of self-rising flour, however, or you can't find it in a gluten-free variety, you can easily transform your all-purpose flour into self-rising flour. Here's how.

For every 1 cup of all-purpose flour required, add the following.

1 ½ tsp. baking powder

¼ tsp. salt

Mix ingredients thoroughly with a fork. You may also need to adjust the recipe somewhat by decreasing the total amount of flour by 2 teaspoons per cup (which is replaced with the baking powder and salt).

That's it! Now don't you feel like a baking pro?

Blueberry Cobbler

My favorite dessert is my mother-in-law's blueberry cobbler. It's sweet without being too sweet, and it has the perfect bread-to-fruit ratio that makes this dessert a true comfort food.

When I make this cobbler, I use a gluten-free flour mix and substitute the sugar with ½ cup of honey. It's delicious either way.

1. Preheat oven to 375°F.

2. Rub oil into a small skillet.

3. In a large bowl, mix together the flour, sugar, milk, and butter. Pour the batter into the skillet. Add the blueberries on top. (The batter will rise through the blueberries while baking.)

4. Bake for 40 minutes or until cobbler is golden brown. Serve hot with a cup of tea or coffee.

2 tsp. oil (for the pan)

1 cup self-rising flour

¾ cup sugar

1 cup milk

6 Tbsp. butter, melted

2 cups frozen blueberries

HOMEMADE WHIPPED CREAM

Make your dessert extra special by topping it with homemade whipped cream.

1 16-oz. carton heavy whipping cream

¼ cup sugar

1 tsp. vanilla extract

Pinch of salt

Combine ingredients in a large bowl. Beat on high using a hand mixer until peaks form. Apply liberally to all desserts.

Apple Pie

Nothing says Americana like a good ol' fashioned apple pie—but who has time to make it from scratch? Instead, make yours semi-homemade by using store-bought crusts and apple pie filling. You'll enjoy the smell of it baking in the oven, and it'll taste just as good as if you spent hours in the kitchen.

Store-bought crusts are usually 9 inches in diameter, so a small, 9-inch skillet would work best. If you need to use a larger skillet, though, buy an extra pie crust and use it to fill in the gaps on the top and bottom crusts.

---

1. Preheat oven to 400°F.

2. Rub oil into a small skillet. Place one pie shell in the skillet.

3. In a large bowl, stir the cinnamon and nutmeg into the apple pie filling if desired. Add the pie filling to the skillet.

4. Cut slits into the second pie shell and place it on top of apple pie filling. (The slits ensure the heat can escape without causing the filling to bubble over.) Brush the egg white onto the pie shell so it can bake to a beautiful golden brown.

5. Bake 40 minutes or until crust is nice and golden.

2 tsp. oil (for the pan)

2 frozen pie crusts (defrosted)

1 tsp. cinnamon (optional)

1 tsp. nutmeg (optional)

2 21-oz. cans apple pie filling

1 egg white

Modern Cast Iron

Apple Crisp

If you like the flavor of apple pie but want to make a healthier, gluten-free version, try this recipe for Apple Crisp. Although some crisp recipes call for tart apples, I recommend using sweet ones because you won't need to use as much sugar. You can also mix things up a bit by using different varieties of apples or by cutting the apples into different size chunks instead of thin slices.

_____

1. Preheat oven to 350°F.

2. Rub oil into a large skillet and add the sliced apples.

3. In a small bowl, whisk together the honey and apple juice until combined. Stir in the lemon juice, cornstarch, cinnamon, and allspice. Pour the mixture in the skillet, tossing the apples to coat them thoroughly. Bake for 20 minutes.

4. Meanwhile, prepare the crisp topping. In a large bowl, combine the oats, flour, pecans, sugar, and salt. Add the melted butter and yogurt and stir the mixture until it's moistened throughout.

5. After the apples have baked for 20 minutes, give them a stir. Add the crisp topping to the skillet by spooning dollops of the mixture over the apples. Bake for an additional 25–30 minutes or until the top is golden brown.

6. Let the crisp rest for 5–10 minutes. Serve hot with vanilla ice cream.

APPLE FILLING

½ Tbsp. oil (for the pan)

2 lb. apples (5–7 apples), peeled and sliced ¼ inch thick

⅓ cup honey

¼ cup apple juice

1 Tbsp. lemon juice

1 Tbsp. cornstarch

½ tsp. ground cinnamon

¼ tsp. ground allspice

CRISP TOPPING

1 cup old-fashioned oats

½ cup almond flour

½ cup chopped pecans (optional)

⅓ cup brown sugar

Pinch of salt

4 Tbsp. unsalted butter, melted

¼ cup plain yogurt

Brownies

I don't know anyone who makes brownies from scratch. There are just too many delicious easy-to-make mixes out there to choose from, including organic, vegan, and gluten-free options. But if you're still making your brownies in a square baking pan, you're missing out on the crispy-edge goodness that comes with baking in cast iron.

Instead of giving you a complicated brownie recipe, I recommend using your favorite store-bought mix and simply baking it in a cast-iron skillet. The heavy pan will give you nice, crispy edges while keeping the inside perfectly gooey. Just remember that cast iron retains heat more than traditional brownie pans, so you may need to lower the baking temperature by a few degrees or reduce the cook time. Most mixes list various temperatures and cook times on the back of the box; go with the ones recommended for darker pans. However, since the brownies will continue to cook for a few minutes after you remove the skillet from the oven, you may want to reduce your cook time by an additional 3–5 minutes. For an extra crispy bottom, preheat the skillet before adding the brownie mix.

To give your brownies some homemade flair, add chopped nuts and serve with vanilla ice cream. And, of course, serve the brownies in the hot skillet. Everyone will enjoy the fun dessert, and no one will care that it didn't take you all day to make it.

Cooking with Cast Iron

Skillet Cookie Cake

When I was little, my family owned a cookie store in our local mall. For years, my birthday cakes were giant chocolate chip cookies with "Happy Birthday" written in colored icing. To this day, I love giant cookies (or cookies of any size, really).

If you like cookies as much as I do, you'll love this Skillet Cookie Cake. It's the perfect crossover between flat, crispy cookies and tall, fluffy cakes. You can still use icing to write "Happy Birthday" on it, but a generous portion of vanilla ice cream will do nicely. Candles are optional.

---

1. Preheat oven to 375°F. Place a large skillet in the oven to preheat.

2. Pour melted butter into a bowl. Add the sugars, salt, and vanilla, and whisk together. Add the eggs, and whisk again until the mixture is smooth.

3. In a separate bowl, mix together the flour and baking soda. Add the flour mixture to the butter mixture, and stir until combined. Then stir in the chocolate chips and nuts.

4. Remove the skillet from the oven, and rub oil into it using tongs and paper towels. Pour batter into the hot skillet, using a spatula to even it out.

5. Bake the cookie for about 20 minutes or until edges are golden brown. Let the skillet sit for 15 minutes. Serve warm in the skillet with vanilla ice cream.

12 Tbsp. unsalted butter, melted

½ cup sugar

¾ cup packed dark brown sugar

1 tsp. salt

2 tsp. vanilla

2 eggs

1 ¾ cup all-purpose flour

½ tsp. baking soda

1 cup chocolate chips

1 cup pecans, chopped (optional)

½ Tbsp. oil (for the pan)

Conclusion

I wrote this book while I was pregnant with my son, Gordon. As my waistline expanded, I spent countless hours in the kitchen testing recipes (and eating the results!), and even more time at the computer writing and researching cookware. My patient husband Robby drove me to Jacksonville—a three-hour trip each way—multiple times to meet with the food photographer. When I was seven months pregnant, Robby drove seven hours to take me to the Lodge foundry. And I put the finishing touches on this book while Gordon napped on a pillow in my lap.

Why would I put so much effort into a simple book on cast iron? Because to me, cast iron isn't just cookware. It's a tangible link to the traditions of our grandparents and forefathers.

Over the past few months, as I've alternated between preparing this book and preparing for a new baby, such family traditions have become even more important to me. I want my son to know how his great-grandparents lived—that they didn't have much, but they made do and were content with what they had. I want Gordon to appreciate the time and effort that goes into a home-cooked meal. And I want him to enjoy our time around the table, whether it's for an easy weeknight dinner or a big family get-together.

It's true that simply cooking meals in a cast-iron pan won't accomplish any of this. But if I tell Gordon about his family, if I share the history, if I encourage him to embrace the cast-iron traditions of the past, then maybe, just maybe, he'll come to understand what I now know: one of the most valuable things in life is time spent with loved ones around the table.

I hope you share this truth—and lots of great cast-iron dinners—with those you love.

Gordon Jones, one day old.

Index

accessories, 34–36
advantages of cast iron, 25–26
appetizers, 110–115
    Layered Nachos, 113
    Spinach Casserole, 114

beef
    Beef & Vegetable Soup, 139
    Beef Pot Roast, 185–186
    Beef Stroganoff, 160
    Creamy Pot Roast, 186
    Fajitas, 156–157
    Grilled Roast Beef Sandwich with Smoked
        Cheddar Cheese, 147
    Ground Beef Stroganoff, 160
    Layered Nachos, 113
    Mary Frances's Taco Soup, 141
    Meatloaf, 187–188
    Mini Meatloaves, 188
    Saucy Fajitas, 157
    Shepherd's Pie, 191
    Sloppy Joe, 149
    Stay-at-Home Steak, 154–155
    Tater Tot Shepherd's Pie, 191
biscuits
    Buttermilk Pour Biscuits, 100
    Buttermilk Skillet Biscuit, 100
    Mayonnaise Biscuits, 103
    Mayonnaise Rolls, 103
    Traditional Biscuits, 98
breakfast
    Bacon, 86
    Blueberry Compote, 87

    Eggs, 83
    Grand Slam, 81–83
    Pancakes, 87
    Peach Dutch Baby, 91
    Robby's Quiche, 93
    Sausage & Gravy, 84

chicken
    Baked Chicken, 177
    Baked Chicken Tenders, 153
    Chicken Alfredo (variation on Sausage
        Alfredo), 163
    Chicken & Yellow Rice, 178
    Chicken Pot Pie, 180
    Crispy Coconut Chicken Tenders, 153
    Easiest Chicken Pot Pie, 181
    Panfried Chicken, 175
    Southern Fried Chicken, 173–175
cleaning methods, 55–56
cooktops, 78
cookware alternatives
    aluminum pans, 43–44
    chemical nonstick pans, 41–42
    copper pans, 45
    stainless steel, 43, 45
cornbread
    Corn Muffins, 108–109
    Corn Pone, 105
    Cornsticks, 108–109
    Hoe Cakes, 105–106
    johnnycakes (or journey cakes), 105–106
    Southern Cornbread, 108
    Sweetened Cornbread, 109

deglazing, 117
desserts
    Apple Crisp, 203
    Apple Pie, 199
    Blueberry Cobbler, 198
    brownies, 204
    Homemade Whipped Cream, 198
    Skillet Cookie Cake, 207

gluten-free substitutions, 74–75, 195

health benefits vs. alternative cookware,
    41–45
history of cast iron, 15–16

Lodge Manufacturing, 17–21

manufacturing process, 15, 17–20
minimalism, 77

oil
    for cooking, 63, 65
    for seasoning, 61, 63
    smoke points, 62
ovens, 78, 80–81

pasta
    Alfredo Sauce, 162
    Homemade Mac & Cheese, 125
    Beef Stroganoff, 160
    Ground Beef Stroganoff, 160
    Sausage Alfredo, 163
pork
    Bean & Sausage Soup, 142
    Grown-Up Grilled Ham & Cheese, 146–147
    Sausage Alfredo, 163
    Sausage & Cabbage, 192

potatoes
    Bacon and Cheese Potatoes, 126
    Garlic Potatoes, 126
preheating the oven, 96

restoration methods
    baking, 69
    dissolving, 66, 69
    scouring, 66
rice
    Shirley's Rice, 131
    Chicken & Yellow Rice, 178

sandwiches
    Grilled Roast Beef Sandwich with Smoked
        Cheddar Cheese, 147
    Grown-Up Grilled Ham & Cheese, 146–147
    Sloppy Joe, 149
sausage
    Bean & Sausage Soup, 142
    Sausage Alfredo, 163
    Sausage & Cabbage, 192
seafood
    Salmon Cakes, 168
    Salmon with Artichokes, 167
    Scallops Alfredo (variation on Sausage
        Alfredo), 163
    Shrimp Alfredo (variation on Sausage
        Alfredo), 163
seasoning (cooking)
    Better than Bouillon Beef Base, 117
    Better than Bouillon Chicken Base , 117
    Morton's Nature's Seasons Seasoning
        Blend (ingredients list), 75
    Lawry's Seasoned Salt (ingredients list), 75
    Cavender's All Purpose Greek Seasoning
        (ingredients list), 75
    Taco Seasoning, 111

seasoning (nonstick finish)
    deep seasoning method, 51
    defined, 49
    fried-egg challenge, 54
    light seasoning method, 50–51
    preseasoned, 20, 53
    science of seasoning, 49–50
side items
    Baby Limas, 121
    Collard Greens, 118
    Coleslaw, 152
    Creamed Spinach, 162
    Field Peas, 122
    Garlic Potatoes, 126
    Homemade Mac & Cheese, 125
    Maduros (plantains), 135
    Papa's Sweet Potato Casserole, 132
    Sautéed Asparagus, 129
    Shirley's Rice, 131
soups
    Beef & Vegetable Soup, 139
    Mary Frances's Taco Soup, 141
    Bean & Sausage Soup, 142
storing cast iron, 57
stove, cast-iron, 8–9
syrup making, 9–10

troubleshooting cast iron, 58, 60
types of cast iron
    bakeware, 28
    bare cast iron, 26–29, 31–33
    cornbread pans, 27
    Dutch ovens, 28–29, 32–33
    enamel cookware, 28–29, 32–33
    furniture, 15, 32
    griddles, 27
    grill pans, 27
    kettles, 8-11, 14–15
    lightweight, 31
    rust resistant, 29
    skillets, 17, 26

vegetables
    Baby Limas, 121
    Coleslaw, 152
    Collard Greens, 118
    Creamed Spinach, 162
    Eggplant Parmesan, 171
    Field Peas, 122
    Maduros (plantains), 135
    Papa's Sweet Potato Casserole, 132